Master Your Memory With Dr. Amazing

How Not to Forget

The Ultimate Memory Improvement Training Program

By
Dr. Amazing
"World's Leading Memory Expert"

Written by M. Teitelbaum, M.D., J.D., also known as Dr. Amazing.

Canadian Cataloguing in Publication Data

Teitelbaum, M.
  Master your memory with Dr. Amazing

  Includes index.
  ISBN 1-55212-252-2

  1. Mnemonics. I. Title.
BF385.T34 1999   153.1'4   C99-910563-9

TRAFFORD

This book was published *on-demand* in cooperation with Trafford Publishing.
On-demand publishing is a unique process and service of making a book available for retail sale to the public taking advantage of on-demand manufacturing and Internet marketing.
On-demand publishing includes promotions, retail sales, manufacturing, order fulfilment, accounting and collecting royalties on behalf of the author.

Suite 6E - 2333 Government St., Victoria, BC, Canada V8T 4P4

Phone	250-383-6864	Toll-free	1-888-232-4444 (Canada & US)
Fax	250-383-6804	E-mail	sales@trafford.com
Web site	www.trafford.com	TRAFFORD PUBLISHING IS A DIVISION OF TRAFFORD HOLDINGS LTD.
Trafford Catalogue #99-0021		www.trafford.com/robots/99-0021.html

10   9   8   7   6   5   4   3

ACKNOWLEDGMENTS

For some of the humor at the head of chapters I thank Edward Carroll, Dennis Taylor, Ron Langill, Dean Inge, P.J. Enright, and Tony Davie.

For assistance I thank Ellen Dubin, Lori Elmelund, Wayne Allyn Root, Hope Garber, and my stepdaughters, Carla and Starr Andreeff.

A major job of editing was performed by my son, Bruce.

Special thanks to Wayne Lundberg for his excellent chapter on Mapping for Memory.

Not only for her help in writing and editing, but also for her enduring support, my heartfelt thanks and love to my wife, Helen.

Book Also Written by Dr. Amazing

Hypnosis Induction Technics

Audiocassettes Written and Recorded by Dr. Amazing

Learn How Not to Forget

A series of four instructional tapes supplementing this book and making it much easier to improve your memory. Please see the last page of this book for purchasing information.

FORWARD

I once read about a man in South India who, in 1886, was able to simultaneously keep in mind and do the following eleven things and afterwards correctly repeat the whole[1].

1. Play a game of chess without seeing the board.

2. Without seeing the chess board, direct the movement of a knight so that it should make the circuit of the board within the outline of a horse traced on it, and enter no other squares than those.

3. Carry on a conversation upon various subjects.

4. Complete a Sanskrit verse from the first line given him.

5. Multiply five figures by a multiplier of four figures.

6. Add a sum of three columns, each of eight rows of figures.

7. Commit to memory a Sanskrit verse of sixteen words -- the words being given to him out of their order and at the option of the tester.

8. Keep count of the strokes of a bell rung by another.

9. Commit to memory two sentences of Spanish given on the same system as No. 7."

10. Complete a "magic square," a square consisting of sixteen inner squares in four rows of four squares each, in which the sums of every group of four added up to the same total, whether tried horizontally or vertically (see illustration below).

11. Complete a second "magic square" with a different total from that of the first magic square.

When I first read about this, many years ago, I was amazed, but I was not yet "Dr. Amazing." How could anyone tackle these feats and do them at the same time?

Recently, I went back and re-considered the Indian's feats. I realized that when I perform on the stage I do more than he did with some of those acts, although not all at the same time. I developed this ability by following the principles of memorization which are detailed in this book.

The Indian expert could do his "magic square" with two magic squares successively. I have performed blindfolded two magic squares simultaneously.

I not only cause all the squares in each column and each row to add up to a magic number previously selected by the audience, but additionally I make the diagonals, the four corner squares and the four center squares also add up to that magic number.

This is an example of a magic square in which each set of four squares adds up to 47.

5	17	17	8
17	8	11	11
10	13	15	9
15	9	4	19

CHESS ANYONE?

I don't know whether the Indian expert was allowed to land his knight on the same square of a chessboard more than once when outlining the horse traced on it. But I easily can move a knight around so that it lands on each of the 64 squares of the board but one time, starting the knight from any square chosen by the audience, and I can do it blindfolded. I have on occasion worked with two chess boards simultaneously.

Does this sound impressive? Well, it certainly impresses the audience and leaves them scratching their heads.

What is even more amazing is that *anyone* of average intelligence can perform these seemingly impossible feats!

If I could improve my untrained memory to perform these memory acts, YOU CAN TOO! All the tools needed are in this book, and this book has a lot more. I invite you to learn what I know.

TRAIN THE BRAIN

This book will assist you in increasing your ability to absorb information, to retain it and to recall it. By utilizing daily the methods I will describe, and stressing your memory by placing a greater load on it, you will find that your memory will not disappoint you. In fact, it will enrich your life.

And no matter from what level you start, and no matter how old you are, you can and will improve your memory.

With a better memory will come satisfaction, confidence and the ability to continue improving your memory. Barring illness, drugs or injury, the only obstacle to improving your memory is a lack of desire.

Why do you want to improve your memory? Although a good one doesn't equate with intelligence, it is very difficult to think if you don't have a store of information in your mind.

Using the magic of improved memory, you not only will have a lot of fun impressing your friends and associates, but you will gain a terrific asset for enriching your life, socially and economically.

I have read nearly every book on memory and am familiar with all published memory systems. I have polished and improved upon those which have some value, and invented a few of my own. I am convinced I am providing you with the most advanced and user-friendly memory methods in existence.

Learn and enjoy!

Reference 1. *Mind and Memory Training*, Ernest E. Wood,
Occult Research Press, 1939, Chapter XIX.

PERCEPTION, REASON, MEMORY

PERCEPTION, REASON, MEMORY
Form in the mind a Trinity;
Each has its special work to do--
Depending on the other two.

PERCEPTION is the open door
Through which the mind receives its store,
Which REASON classifies, defines,
And to its place each fact assigns.

While MEMORY, with book and pen,
Takes an account of where and when,
And how, each treasure rich is stored--
Nor is the least by her ignored.

When REASON would a truth reveal,
She must to MEMORY appeal,
Who quickly to the written page
Turns, then unlocks the vault of age,

And brings from some safe niche or nook
The fact recorded in the book;
She locks the door; the key she holds;
Her hand alone the vault unfolds.

PERCEPTION might all knowledge gain;
REASON to the highest skill attain;
Yet all of no avail would be,
Should MEMORY misplace her key.

A. S. Boyd, 1886

MASTER YOUR MEMORY WITH DR. AMAZING

HOW NOT TO FORGET

CONTENTS

CHAPTER ONE

SOMETHING TO REMEMBER

The best way for a man to remember his
wedding anniversary is to forget it... just once.

Shakespeare had a vocabulary of twenty-five thousand words. If his wife told him to pick up twenty-five items at the supermarket, could he have done it without notes? I doubt it.

What is <u>memory</u>? It is the recall into your conscious mind of past observations and concepts. If you had no memory, you would have no knowledge of time, place or person. You would not know where you are or who you are. You would not know about pleasure or pain, sadness or happiness. You wouldn't even be able to read, since you would have no alphabet, and you would not understand the spoken word since you wouldn't know what each word represents.

Can you imagine how frustrated you would be if just a part of your memory was lost? What if you forgot where you lived or where the toilet was?

A memory is essential for normal living and a good memory is mandatory for success.

Memory is a result of how we absorb and store information to be available for later recall. <u>Recall</u> is the retrieval from the subconscious mind of the stored information. Memory is not the equivalent of intelligence. Intelligence is determined by how we use the stored information.

There are three kinds of memory. Semantic memory is comprised of the vast network of associations and concepts that underlie our general knowledge of the world. It includes what you learned in school and from the media and what you observed. Although some of this information drops out of memory, the total of semantic memory increases with age.

Episodic memory is personal to the individual. What movies you have seen, what you had to eat yesterday, who you dated. It allows us to recollect specific incidents from our past. This type of memory will decline with age and it is subject to replacement by more recent memories. You might remember what you had for dinner last night, but not what you ate a week ago Friday.

Implicit memory deals with body functions. It is a procedural memory which allows us to learn skills and know how to do things. Even though you have not roller-skated or typed for 20 years, your body retains much of those skills.

As we grow older, we tend to forget episodic type information we were recently exposed to. Phone numbers, addresses, names and where we put things seem to drop out of mind. Memories from way back seem to remain intact, although it takes longer to retrieve them - as if the memories had to course along detours to reach the conscious mind.

The decline with age has been attributed to loss of brain cells, reduction of blood supply to the brain, the reduction of the amount of the chemical neurotransmitters which carry the signals from one brain cell to another, and even to the use of different parts of the brain by older people.

But a major cause of decreased memory function has been ignored by many. It is simply disuse. The function of any body part will decrease if it is not used.

"Use it or lose it" appropriately applies to exercising to maintain muscle tone and bone strength, and it applies equally to all other body systems and functions, including memory. Memory will decrease with disuse and it will increase with use and stress.

Regardless of your current ability to remember, it can be improved. If we put a greater load on memory and improve how we absorb information, we will increase retention and recall.

I CAN STILL REMEMBER

Many years ago, I wondered if my brain was made of Teflon - like the cookware of the same name, nothing stuck. I couldn't remember names or faces. I didn't know how to take notes or organize material. I seemed to forget facts shortly after I thought I had learned them, and I envied some of my friends who could reel off reams of statistics. Ultimately, I had no choice but to decide not to remain a failure.

Think back to when you forgot a name three seconds after being introduced to someone. What about when you "knew" an historical date, the name of an inventor or a geometry formula, but couldn't think of it in time to answer the question on a school test?

How about when you were in a group of people and some "know-it-all" spouted off the names of the supreme court justices or all the films of Elizabeth Taylor? Did you feel inadequate? Did you believe your memory was not very good, and you had to be careful not to expose your mental weakness?

Pssst! Your memory potential was probably as good as the know-it-all's. It's just that you never had the interest to learn the names of the supreme court justices or Elizabeth Taylor's films.

You may not have a good memory for remembering names or faces, or for remembering geometry, but I'll wager that in certain areas your memory excels. Just think of your hobbies and what you know about your collections. If you listen to music, think of all the musical artists you can name.

People who astound us with remarkable memories for names of everyone working for them, or stock prices going back for years, or quarterback records, or batting statistics have special interest in those areas. They seem like memory experts. But their memories in other areas might be minimal. They have excelled in one area because they have developed an interest in the subject matter.

SIMPLE TOOLS OF MEMORY

There's hardly a person who doesn't already use some memory tools such as key words, acronyms, acrostics, jingles and verses.

Key Words are words that instantly cause us to recall something to which they are associated. "June" might cause us to think of a bride. "Christmas" relates to Christmas trees, Santa Claus and snow.

Acronyms are words formed from the first letters or syllables of other words, as in ETA for estimated time of arrival, NATO for North Atlantic Treaty Organization, and NFL for National Football League.

Acrostics are arrangements of words in which the first or last letter in each line, taken in order, spell a phrase. To remember the notes on the lines of the treble clef (EGBDF), music students transpose the notes to "Every Good Boy Does Fine." In this case, the acrostic is the reverse of the acronym - the phrase recalls the letters instead of the letters recalling the phrase.

Jingles for use in retention are repetitions of sounds, as in alliteration (the repetition of the same sounds or a group of letters in a group of words) or rhyme, such as in "He would not retract his attack on the action of the faction."

<u>Verses or Poems</u> consist of arrangements of words in lines usually with regularly repeated accent and often with rhyme.

HOW DOES ONE CLIMB A TEN FOOT WALL?

When I started working on my memory, I wondered when if ever I would be able to remember the key words, jingles, acronyms, and verses I composed to recall numbers, names, historical events, English prose -- the list was endless. My thought processes were interrupted many times by needing to lean over and glance at my notes to recall a word or a phrase. It could take a half a day to work my way through a story which I had already summarized and outlined with key words. I thought I could never do it.

But after I mastered a "cue system alphabet" (hang on, we'll get there), I was retaining the essence of the material in a mere few minutes. How wonderful a feeling it was!

WHO HAS THE POOR MEMORY?

Think back just to yesterday. You probably can't remember in detail more than one percent of everything you saw. It's because 99% went into your <u>immediate</u> (<u>ultra-short term</u> or <u>working</u>) memory, where it faded away in seconds or minutes and did not reach <u>recent</u> (<u>short-term</u>) memory, where you have the ability to acquire and retain new information and can repeat the material after a brief delay. You had no intent to place the forgotten material into your <u>remote</u> (<u>long-term</u>), (<u>permanent</u>) memory because it was irrelevant to your life.

What were the colors of the cars parked in front of your house today? What was your co-worker wearing? At what intersections did you stop your car for traffic lights on the way to work? You saw all these things, but if you don't remember them, it's because you didn't observe them; you had no intent to remember them, no effective system for remembering them at all.

SEEING WITHOUT INTEREST IS NOT BANKABLE

Before information* can be registered or encoded in the brain, it first must be observed through at least one of our senses. Observation is seeing, hearing or feeling with interest.

To be effective, the observation needs to be achieved with the intent to remember. If you decide you want to remember something, and you concentrate your attention to that task, you have taken the most important step toward the accumulation and retention of knowledge.

If the same observation is repeated, either actually through the senses, or by a thought process, the brain's chemical connections are reinforced and the item observed will be transmitted more quickly to its storage cells, where it will be recognized by them as a thought previously received.

NO INTERFERENCE, PLEASE

Interference is any sensory input coming from something other than the desired material. If you want to be a good observer, and have a good memory, you need to be able to focus on the subject at hand without interference. Putting yourself in a place and position for complete concentration without interference is essential.

So turn off the television and make yourself comfortable - just not too comfortable that you fall asleep - in a room without distractions.

Get ready to focus!

----

*Footnote 1:

I use the words item, material and information interchangeably in this book to refer to any event, object, concept, name, organism, thought or sensory stimulus which is capable of being remembered.

KEEPING IT IN MIND

After the registration of sensory input through observation, the next step is retention.

Retention is the storing within the brain of observed material which is capable of being retrieved into the conscious mind at a future time.

Retention of sensory input is increased through 1) repetition, 2) association, and 3) organization.

1) Repetition, the primary method of memorization, results in reinforcement and recognition. It is the simplest way of storing information in the brain.

Although you might repeat information over and over during a single day, retention will be weak. If you repeat the information over a series of days, and then periodically to refresh your memory, retention will be enhanced.

Additionally, the more senses involved in the absorption process, the more deeply the information is impressed into your memory. By reading aloud, you use the senses of seeing and hearing. If at the same time you write down the information, a sixth sense - the kinesthetic sense of position, movement and tension of parts of the body - also is involved.

Don't scoff at reading aloud. We have had speech for 4 million years, but we have had written language for only 4,000 years. We were biologically destined to speak but not to read or write. But reading also involves sound. The brain reads primarily by translating written characters into phonological building blocks of spoken language. Secondarily, it links a memorized picture of a complete written word to its meaning, recalling it in a way that bypasses the need to sound out the word. Hence, reading aloud assists the primary brain path for reading to forge stronger links of memory.

When you repeat aloud the lists or concepts included in this book, be sure to concentrate on what you say. Hearing is not enough if you don't really listen to yourself.

ASSOCIATION IS NOT A DIRTY WORD

2) Association is the relating of two or more items to each other. When items have been associated, the thought of one will tend to recall the others. Our brains subconsciously make most of the associations.

Recall is based on something in your conscious mind - an event, an object, a concept, a name, a face, etc. - which brings into awareness another item by associating with it. There can be no recall without the association of that observed material or conscious thought with the item to be recalled from our memory.

For example: Jim lives on Elm Street in Lima, Ohio. He drives by Elm Street in Dayton. Seeing the street sign can immediately cause him to recall his own street, and then his house, and then his wife and family. They are all in his memory bank and are brought to his conscious thought by the thread of association. The thread of associated thoughts might continue on and on, but it usually is interrupted by a new external stimulus to the conscious mind.

The stimulus to recall need not be visual. A certain scent or a song or a touch or a taste might take you back in time, starting a new thread of associated thoughts.

ORGANIZATION IS NOT JUST FOR UNIONS

3) Organization. Just as we stack certain dishes in different parts of kitchen cabinets, rather than scattering them about, we organize information in our heads for ease of learning and retention. To effectively achieve organization, we use the processes of summarization, outlining and classification.

Summarization is the making of a brief statement about the content of a topic.

Outlining is the listing of the important points of a series of topics.

Classification is the grouping together of like materials into categories.

Intentional classification of large amounts of information usually requires the material to be first summarized and outlined.

Books generally are good examples of organization because they routinely include like information in the same chapter and an index provides the outline and the classification.

In Chapter Nine I will expand upon the subject of organization of materials.

ARTIFICIAL DEVICES

For better recall, most of us have used simple artificial or mechanical methods to make stronger associations. Who didn't learn the jingle, "i after e except after c..." when studying spelling in elementary school?

Remember - of course you do - the verse:

"Thirty days hath September,

April, June and November.

All the rest have thirty-one

Excepting February alone..."

What about tying a string around a finger to remind us of something to do? Do you place the garbage bag next to the front door, so you won't forget to take it out?

These simple memory systems are very effective. Shortly, we will proceed to the more advanced memory systems.

Despite repetition, association, organizing the material and utilizing memory systems, memories still will fade if they are not refreshed. If you don't revisit your memories, they will be lost through the passage of time.

SUCCESS OR FAILURE - CHOOSE ONE

Success will be yours, but only if you motivate yourself to learn every concept presented here and to practice every day the methods illustrated.

Success will be yours if you keep in the front of your mind the desire to take every opportunity to utilize the skills and techniques you will gain from my experience.

Success will be yours, and you will become a monarch of memory - a mnemonist. ("Pronounced "knee-monist.") The word is derived from Mnemosyne, the Greek goddess of memory. A mnemonist is a person who utilizes better memory systems than you have up to now.

Suggestion: Right now, pencil in on your daily calendar the times you will devote to improving your memory. Yes, do it right now. I'll wait.

Did you pencil in your calendar as I suggested? If you didn't, you should not be reading on. Go do it.

Henry was driving Joe and their wives to dinner.
Joe, a victim of Alzheimer's, was in front with
Henry. Joe said he and his wife saw a great
movie last week. "What was the name?" asked Henry.
Joe said, "I don't remember, but I have a
unique memory system. What's the name of
the flower that blooms in the spring and has
thorns?" "A rose," Henry answered. "That's it,"
said Joe. Joe turns to the back and says,
"Rose, what was the name of the movie
we saw last week?"

CHAPTER TWO

ASSOCIATIONS

"Doc, I forget. Do I have Alzheimer's or not?"

P.J. Enright

I'm going to list ten objects for you. Silently read the list one time, close the book, count to fifty aloud, then write on your sheet of paper as many of the objects as you can remember. Then re-open the book.

Computer

Bagpipes

Suitcase

Thermometer

Carpet

Oak tree

Rainbow

Elephant

Peanuts

Garden hose

TEST TIME

Now close the book, count to fifty and write your list. Don't go back and peak! CLOSE THE BOOK!

This paragraph is reserved for me to listen to music while you take the test.

Okay, you're back with me. How many did you get right?

Seven is a good score. If you scored ten, maybe you should join me when I lecture or do my memory stage shows. But scoring seven or more is not the entire test. Did you have them in the correct order?

THE CASE OF THE DISAPPEARING WORDS

Let's analyze what just occurred. This is an example of accessing immediate memory. Immediate memory also is known as working memory and as ultra short-term memory. This ability to remember information for seconds and maybe for a few minutes does not decline with age. Unfortunately, the information that goes into immediate memory does rapidly fade. Tomorrow, you'll be lucky to remember three items from the list.

You read each item, but the list was in a vacuum. You had nothing to relate it to, so you had no clues to assist you in recalling the specific items. You also had no way to remember which one was fifth on the list or which one was number nine.

In addition, I introduced the concept of displacement. While the natural process of fading caused some of the items to vanish from your memory, I displaced some objects from your memory by having you count the numbers from one to fifty. Concentrating your mind on the numbers allowed them to replace some of the objects in your immediate memory.

And another thing: memories are not static. Not only can they be lost through fading or replaced completely through displacement, but they can be changed through expansion (padding) because when there is a memory gap or when part of a memory is lost, the mind tends to fill in the blank with something which seems logical, even if it is not true.

A somewhat similar process occurs when we retell a prior experience still in memory, but some details are changed or enlarged upon. This process is called <u>reconstruction</u>. The longer the period of time from the event to the relating of it and the more times the event is related, the greater the reconstruction.

The operation of expanding memory or its reconstruction are two of the reasons why observers of an event will give different versions of it. If instead of being an observer, one is part of the event, more of the original memory is likely to be retained.

So there you have it. It is a myth that memories are true recordings of past events.

If you don't make any associations with items, if some items are allowed to fade, if other thoughts enter your mind before you have utilized a method to remember, if your mind substitutes a "memory" for a lost one - your memory of many, if not all, of the items is lost.

EXTERNAL AIDS TO MEMORY

Note taking is an important factor in improving memory because the notes are not affected by reconstruction, fading or displacement.

If you don't take good notes either by hand or by voice recording of material you want to remember such as lectures or names of people, you will have no means of refreshing your memory. Get in the habit of carrying a notebook and pen with you and write down those things you want to remember or use a tape recorder.

LET US ASSOCIATE TOGETHER

We touched on the subject of associations in Chapter One. Let's expand upon it.

Aristotle and Thomas Aquinas determined that associations were based on three laws of nature:

1. The <u>Law of Similarity</u>. An impression tends to recall other impressions that are similar to it.

2. The <u>Law of Contrast</u>. An impression also tends to recall impressions opposite to it.

3. The <u>Law of Propinquity</u>. An impression tends to recall other impressions that occurred at the same time or place.

Today, we are aware that associations can be broken down into more specific categories, such as:

Rhymers or Soundalikes: Hat, bat, cat, rat, chat, fat, mat, gnat, pat, sat and vat.

Synonyms: Words which do not sound alike but have similar meanings such as connect, associate, attach, cohere, couple, fasten and join.

Neighboring: Objects which are near one another, so that thinking of one reminds us of the other. Refrigerator and oven, school and playground.

Matching Pairs: Things which go together. Bread and butter; socks and shoes; coat and tie; soup and crackers; thunder and lightning.

Antonyms/Opposites: Hot and cold, black and white, beauty and the beast.

Cause and Effect: Overpark and pay a fine; miss your spouse's birthday and you can forget sex; throw a stone into a pond and cause ripples.

General and Specific (genus and species): Roses and American Beauty; buildings and church; doctors and pediatrician.

Whole and Part: Book and page; jury and juror.

Phrase links: Expanding words into catchy phrases. Bill Borge (billboard); Bob Frapples (bob for apples).

There are many other ways our minds automatically associate one object or event with another, but the basis of all memory is that we do associate.

VISUAL ENHANCEMENT METHODS FOR STRONGER ASSOCIATIONS

Visual Enhancement Methods are ways we can change actual observations to be more vivid in our memory and thus make a stronger association. The more bizarre or exaggerated we make observed items in our mind's eye, the better we will remember them. We should make them farcical, zany, ludicrous, outrageous - anything but ordinary.

In working to improve your visual enhancing skills, and thus your memory, keep in mind and practice each of the following methods. They are your tools. Continue to refer to them as you strive to engrave images of objects and concepts into your lifelong memory.

The Amplification Method is a way of enhancement by which we reform the visualized image of any observed item by changing its shape, color, size. Usually we would enlarge the object (exaggeration), but in certain cases we might envision it as being much smaller. For example: Suppose you want to remember a cat. If you imagine the cat to look much larger, and with unusual shape and colors, won't you remember it better?

The Replacement Method works with pairs and it substitutes an unusual object for an ordinary object. This method is normally used when remembering names and faces and you want to attach a memorable object to a face. For example: If you want to remember the face of a man who smokes cigars, it would be customary to visualize him with a cigar in his mouth. But how many other people smoke cigars? If this man were a plumber, wouldn't it be more memorable if you pictured a toilet plunger stuck on top of his head?

The Multiplication Method will enhance memory by visualizing a huge amount or number of the items.

Now let's take the cat and multiply it. If one ludicrous cat is easier to remember than an ordinary cat, aren't a number of ludicrous cats even easier to remember?

The Zany Pose Method places the object in an interesting or zany pose. For example: Seeing the cat holding a triple dip ice cream cone or the cat doing a "paw" stand, would be memorable. The more humorous or nonsensical the image, the more likely you will remember it.

The Action Method places the items in motion, and in a motion not ordinarily seen. For example: If you saw a photo of the Titanic a year ago, you would be hard pressed to pick it out from among photos of a number of ships. But if you saw the movie, a vivid image of the ship might remain in your memory for many years.

The Transformation Method enhances a concept by transforming it into a visual image or object that can represent it - similar to an icon on your computer desktop representing a file or an application.

For example, here's a concept: "When a dog bites man, that is not news, because it happens so often. But if a man bites a dog, that is news." We can transform this into an image. Wouldn't a picture of a man biting a dog help you to remember the concept?

How about visualizing "A stitch in time saves nine." Wouldn't picture of a bulldog on one side of a fence and nine cats on the other side and you "sewing" up the fence hole help you remember the concept?

Think about this. If you had used some of the visual enhancement methods when you read the list at the beginning of this chapter, would you have been able to score higher in recall?

Let us see how you might have visualized two of those ten objects using some of the Visual Enhancement Methods.

Computer

Amplification:	The monitor is in an oval shape rather than rectangular. The screen is red and has teeth like a shark's mouth.
Multiplication:	There are two monitors on the desk
Zany Pose:	The monitors have legs and outstretched arms.
Action:	The monitors are dancing.

Thermometer

Amplification:	It is in the shape of the letter "s." It has a large red fluid container.
Multiplication:	There are three of them.
Zany Pose:	The fluid containers are shaped like smiling faces.
Action:	They are jumping in and out of body orifices.

(The day I wrote this happened to be my birthday. When I woke up, I found my wife's red bra draped on my computer screen. What a great visual enhancement to remembering a computer!)

Now is the time for you to practice visual enhancement. Write down the remaining eight objects and make your own list of enhancements for them. Maybe I'll test you on them later.

FIVE AND ONE MAKES FOR FULL SENSORY ENHANCEMENT

The six methods we just covered were for visual enhancement - the use of just one of our senses.

The All Senses Application brings into play all five external senses, as I have listed them: seeing, hearing, tasting, touching, and smelling. An internal kinesthetic sense (the sensation of position, movement, tension, etc. of parts of the body perceived through nerve-end organs in muscles, tendons and joints) makes six. We tend to rely most heavily on our sense of sight, the kinesthetic sense and to a lesser degree our sense of hearing. However, some people have special aptitudes for the so-called minor senses of taste, touch and smell.

You, too, can better develop the senses of taste, touch and smell. When you visualize an object, imagine how it tastes and smells and feels. Imagine a sound it may make. The more senses you apply to an object, the better you will remember it.

Enough of concepts. Let's see how you handle names and faces...

Patient: Doc, I can't remember anything.

Doctor: How long have you had this problem?

Patient: What problem?

CHAPTER THREE

NAMES AND FACES, FACES AND NAMES

"I never forget a face, but in your case I'll be
glad to make an exception."

Groucho Marx, 1970

We have just covered visually enhancing objects. Now let's apply that concept to faces.

A LOT GOES A LONG WAY

In Chapter Two we found that the more bizarre we make observed items in our mind's eye, the better we will remember them. We should make them farcical, zany, ludicrous, outrageous - anything but ordinary.

Similarly, one of the good ways to improve recall of a face is to exaggerate in a bizarre fashion its most outstanding feature. The more distorted or ludicrous you make that feature, the better you will remember it. If the person has a big nose, you could think of it as humongous. If the person has a ponytail, you could see it as a snake reaching to the floor.

Now go to the mirror, look into it and say aloud, I want to improve my memory for names and faces. Don't ask why. Just go say it three times with meaning and intent. Then come back to the book.

You said it too fast. I didn't have time to brush my teeth.

FACE THE FACTS

If you don't observe what features a person has, how can you go about exaggerating a feature? A necessary step to recalling faces is to observe and determine what features the person has.

What did you observe when you looked in the mirror? Do you think I just wanted you to see your lips move? What did you really observe? What kind of chin do you have? How would you describe your hair and your nose? I know you know what color eyes you have. How about your eyebrows? What shape are they?

Understand the difference between seeing and observing?

If you were to tell a stranger over the phone how he could recognize your face at the airport when you arrive, how would you describe your outstanding features?

How would you describe your mother, sister or spouse so that I would recognize them?

You say you could do it. Okay, go get another sheet of paper and draw your head, and that of members of your family. Draw their faces and their outstanding physical characteristics. You don't have to be an artist, just accentuate what is eye-catching.

WHAT HAVE I HIDDEN?

When you have finished with your drawings, read Appendix B, where I have listed some of the features one should look at when observing a face.

Interesting list? You should commit it to memory. It's your checklist now.

Return to the mirror and check off your features against the list. Does the list help you define your prominent features? Can you now describe yourself to a stranger?

WHAT'S BELOW THE BELT?

Don't get me wrong. I don't believe the only way to remember a person is to look at everything above the neck. It's just that when people talk to us, we usually center our gaze at their mouths, perhaps occasionally glancing at their eyes. We usually stand quite close when we talk to people, so it's difficult to gaze down at the rest of the body without the look being quite noticeable and very suggestive.

People do have stooped shoulders, broad shoulders, hunched backs, inverted chests, barrel chests, large or small breasts, small waists, big hips or bums, fat legs, thin legs, fat ankles and bowed legs. To add details to your image of the people you meet, take time later during the event to look at their bodies from a distance. Note striking physical characteristics, postures and attitudes, and their mannerisms. Do they smoke? How do they hold their cigarettes or purses? Do they have a nervous tick?

Also observe their faces from the side. You may get an entirely different impression from the profile.

If you meet people while they are seated, be sure to look at them later when they are standing. The look can be very different.

You should not put too much reliance on hair styles or color, jewelry, beards or other temporary features. They may change or be absent the next time you see that person. However, neither should you ignore "temporary" features, for they may be permanent for that individual.

With so many things going on when you first talk to someone, it's difficult to cover all the bases, trying to keep the person's name in mind while thinking about analyzing the face or body. But the more you do it, the easier it gets.

WHAT DO I DO FIRST?

Again, I'll make it easier for you. As you get started, don't worry about covering the entire face. Over the span of a few days or a week, just concentrate on one feature, even if it is very ordinary. You could start with hair and hairlines. Get good at classifying the types of hair and shapes of skulls. Using the Visual Enhancement Method, exaggerate the ordinary into the unusual or bizarre, such as red hair being at the end of a mop. Try also putting some action into the hair, such as making waves appear to move like ocean waves or tongues of flame.

After you feel confident in analyzing the hair and scalp while engaging in introductions, spend some time analyzing another part of the head. Keep thinking of it as a game.

Don't limit this practice to new acquaintances. Do it all day long with anyone you can observe, including people on television.

MEET SOME PEOPLE

Here are the names of some people and their most prominent physical characteristic. Make a drawing of how you would visualize each characteristic in a bizarre way. You can use color.

Bob Cook -	Large wide eyes.
Betty Hillman -	Lined forehead.
Esther Kulback -	Thin, stringy grey hair.
Ruth Katchen -	A round face.
Frank Bluestein -	Large ears.
Chester Arron -	Ruddy cheeks.

Save your drawings. I call these <u>fantasy images</u>.

SHOW ME YOU MEAN IT

One more basic before we get on with the teaching of how to remember names.

To demonstrate your intent to learn how to remember names and faces and to put that knowledge into practice, pull out your calendar. What meetings or parties do you have scheduled for the next 30 days? Write "NAMES" in red below each entry to remind you that you will go to the event with the intent to remember many names and faces.

Did you do it? If you didn't, go do it. Don't read any further until you've demonstrated your intent to follow through to be successful with remembering names and faces.

What?? No meetings or parties scheduled? No problem - decide on a local coffee house and prepare to hang out there.

TALK ABOUT BRINGING DOWN THE HOUSE

In 477 B.C. the Greek orator and poet, Simonides, was invited to recite a verse at a large banquet. After the recitation, he was unexpectedly summoned out of the event, and just then the roof of the banquet hall collapsed, crushing beyond recognition all the guests. When Simonides reconstructed the guest list by imagining each location around the tables, he became a hero.

Forgetting names is the number one memory-related complaint. Names - the most difficult aspect of memory and one which has caused much embarrassment. You may become an expert at recalling faces by using the Visual Enhancement Method, but if you can't remember the name that goes with the face, you're still in trouble.

How many times have you gone to a party or a meeting and couldn't remember more than one or two names by the time you arrived home? Would you like to have a dollar for each time you couldn't remember a name, even though the face was familiar?

A face, even without visual enhancement, is still easier to recall than a name because a face requires only recognition. A name is more difficult because when we try to remember it, we have to get a specific piece of information from our memory. And, since you have not yet been trained in making associations with names, you don't have anything in mind to link with the name.

But remembering names is just a skill which can be learned like any other.

WHAT IS A NAME?

Our name is one of our most prized possessions. When people call us by name, we get a good impression of them.

If a mere nodding acquaintance calls you by your name, doesn't it have a warming effect on you?

At the airport, every ticketing clerk and flight attendant has a name badge. When I go to the ticket counter I say, "Hello, Ms. _____. When the flight attendant takes my ticket and I say, "Thank you, _____," I get an appreciative response. You can bet that when I make any special requests, they are going to give me every consideration.

In many restaurants the waiter will greet you and inform you of his name. Ever try telling him your name for fun - and for better service? I do almost every time. You should see the looks on their faces when I say my name. They don't forget to refill my water glass.

FIRST MEETING

What do you do when you meet people for the first time? Your answer most likely will be that you introduce yourself. IT'S THE WRONG THING TO DO. You can state your name, but let them state theirs first. If you go first, you have started that relationship, as brief as it might be, on the wrong foot for several reasons.

1) You have concentrated your attention on giving out your name when you should have been <u>paying attention</u> to the stranger's name and face. The primary reason we do not remember names after a first meeting is that we do not <u>pay attention</u> to them when introduced. <u>Paying attention</u> to the stranger's name should be your first goal when initially meeting anyone. (Do you think I made my point about <u>paying attention?</u>)

2) Most people are self centered. They would rather talk about themselves than listen to others. If you show interest in what they are saying, you will make a much better impression on them.

When I meet someone new, - let's call him Arnold Turrentine - I do not say, "Hi, I am Dr. Amazing." I say, "Hi, what's your name?" Then I have Arnold repeat it by saying, "What did you say?" or "I beg your pardon." In the alternative, I just repeat the name as a question -- "Turrentine?" It really doesn't appear that I am hard of hearing, because usually we are in a crowd, and there is much background noise to justify the request.

Unless the name is as simple as a Smith or a Brown, I then ask Arnold to spell it. I say, "How do you spell Turrentine? This will attract his attention. Invariably, Arnold will spell it out. Why? Because it's important to him, and he wants me to remember it.

At this point I have heard his name pronounced twice and spelled once. It's in my brain beyond short-term memory, where it would remain only for seconds. At least, it's into intermediate memory, where it might remain for hours or for several days.

But I am not done. I haven't even mentioned my name, yet.

Since I have the intent to remember his name, come hell or high water, I say, "Nice to meet you, Arnold Turrentine [or Mr. Turrentine], I am Dr. Amazing." My saying aloud his name tells me that my mind wasn't wandering and the name found some brain cells to stick to. At least long enough that I'll remember it when I leave.

The forgoing interaction doesn't mean that I exclude any other questions or conversation. If the name is out of the ordinary, I might ask, "Did I pronounce Turrentine correctly?" Notice, I repeated the name rather than saying, "Did I pronounce your name correctly?" If the name is of foreign derivation, I could also question the ethnic origin of the name Turrentine, Turrentine's meaning in the other country's language, or how many other Turrentines are in this country. Got the idea?

OTHER CRUTCHES

Since hearing a name utilizes only one of our senses, you should bring into play as many of the other senses as possible. For your vision sense, imagine your writing the person's name across his forehead with a felt-tipped pen. For remembering what the person looks like, pretend you are painting a portrait or taking a snapshot - notice the outstanding features. If the person resembles a well-known person, make the association. Perhaps the names are similar - make the association.

Similarly, if the smell of the person or of the place where you meet is special - make the association. Perhaps the name is related to a taste, such as John Hamburger - make the association.

WHO IN THE HELL ARE YOU?

I can't let Arnold go until I've learned something about him.

After I give my name, I avoid giving Arnold the chance to ask what I do or to comment about my stage career. I focus the conversation on Arnold by following quickly with a question, such as, "How long have you known the host?" or "Where do you live, Mr. Turrentine? This is just to soften him up for my next question: "What do you do, Arnold?" Notice I keep repeating his name. Have you counted how many times up to now?

Well, Arnold is off and running about himself. Not only will I get some background information about him, but I have the opportunity to observe his outstanding physical characteristics. I want to recognize his face the next time I see it.

When it comes time to part, I make use of his name one more time with, "Nice meeting you, Arnold."

Stop! I don't want what I just said to go in and out of your head as if it wasn't important. Not having a routine like mine is the biggest obstacle to remembering names! How are you going to remember the routine if you don't practice it?

So, here and now, take a pen and paper. Write down a basic starting routine, substitute any name, and say it aloud as you write:

1. Hi. What's your name?

2. Arnold Turrentine? or/ What did you say?

3. How do you spell Turrentine?

4. Nice to meet you, Mr. Turrentine , I am _____.

5. How long have you known the host? or/ Where do you live, Mr. Turrentine?

6. What do you do, Mr. Turrentine?

7. Nice meeting you, Arnold.

Say it again three times, then paste it on your bathroom mirror. Every day, repeat it. Before you go to any meeting or party, practice it some more. Substitute a few other questions that might come in handy. You'll need to play it by ear as to how many times you want to repeat the name. Observe reactions and try not to make it apparent that you are just doing the introduction by rote.

SIMONIDES SAYS

Imagine yourself at a business meeting, one at which you've gone around and met a number of people for the first time. You've had them repeat their names and you've repeated them. You've observed them carefully. You've made a conscious effort to remember what they look like. The meeting is over and you leave. What do you do next?

You go to your briefcase or your car and pull out your MEETINGS NOTEBOOK. [Don't buy a cheap one - you should keep it till the day you die.] Date a page and write the name of the meeting, its purpose and where it was held.

Visualize the room to refresh your memory of it. In your mind, visually skim through the meeting as if it were a movie. Picture where people were located and who they were with.

Write the name of every person you met in the order you met them. If you circled a table greeting people, visualize the table. As you recall one person, it will help you remember who was sitting next over.

Beside each name in your notebook, list the person's outstanding feature and what you can remember about their background.

I don't recommend using a card file or a Rolodex file for your list of names, because it is important to place on the same page all the people you meet at an event. Visualizing the event in general helps to recall the specific individuals, and one person tends to recall another, just as Simonides benefitted.

As you record the most prominent feature of the individual, picture in your mind how you exaggerated it in bizarre fashion. If it was too burdensome to memorize the prominent feature during the introduction, this is a good time to think back and do the job of drawing your fantasy images.

GETTING THE PICTURE

You can go home from the meeting, but you are not yet done. Before going to bed, make up words which can substitute for each person's name. Name substitutes can be objects, famous people, animals, places, colors or products - something you can visualize and which will call to mind the name of the person you met. A name substitute which can be so visualized is called a "picture word." Name substitutes also can be words which naturally modify the fantasy image of the person's outstanding feature.

An image which represents a word is called a "word picture."

Recall that in Chapter Two I gave you a list of categories of associations. It included rhymers, synonyms, neighboring pairs, matching pairs, opposites, cause and effect, general and specific, whole and part, abstract and concrete, and phrase links. Name substitutes can be generated from any of these categories of association.

Let's revisit the six people I listed in this chapter and their prominent features. You sketched a fantasy image for each. We can choose name substitutes for them either by coining word pictures or modifying the fantasy images with words that will recall their names.

Just as we visually enhanced their outstanding features to get fantasy images, we can visually enhance substitutes for their names using the visual enhancement methods of amplification, multiplication, zany pose and action.

Here is how I would combine name substitutes with fantasy images.

Bob Cook with large wide eyes - Think of a very tall chef's hat on his head decorated with a pair of yellow hypnotizing eyes. [matching pair - a cook and chef's hat].

Betty Hillman with forehead lines - Visualize her and a man standing in a one of several deep furrows of tilled soil on a hill. [No need for a picture word substitute since hill and man already make good images].

Esther Kulback with thin, stringy hair - Imagine her hair to be icicles. Water drips from them onto her back. [rhymer - Kul and cold; matching pair - cold and icicle].

Ruth Katchen with a round face - Picture her face as a large colored beach ball as she opens the refrigerator in the kitchen. [general and specific - kitchen and refrigerator; rhymer - kitchen and katchen].

Frank Bluestein with large ears - See him as a donkey with large blue ears. The donkey is drinking beer from a stein. [No need for a substitute for blue and stein].

Chester Arron with ruddy cheeks - Visualize an arrow sticking out of one of the apples stuck on his cheek and juice pouring out of the apple. [rhymer - arrow and arron].

Got the idea?

The next time I meet Bob Cook, his eyes will trigger a vision of a pair of hypnotizing eyes on a chef's hat. Ah, chef/cook. "Hi, Mr. Cook."

And when I bump into Frank Bluestein and note his large ears, it'll be easy. I'll associate his ears with a donkey with blue ears drinking beer out of a stein.

The sketches you make combining the name substitute and the fantasy image for the visually enhanced outstanding feature should be images that are memorable.

Our new friend, Arnold Turrentine, relates well to turpentine. I see a can of turpentine and I can smell the odor. I'm using an additional sense - smell.

I call these combined sketches of name substitutes and fantasy images of visually enhanced outstanding features "ringers" - from the expression "dead ringers."

This is a diagram of a ringer:

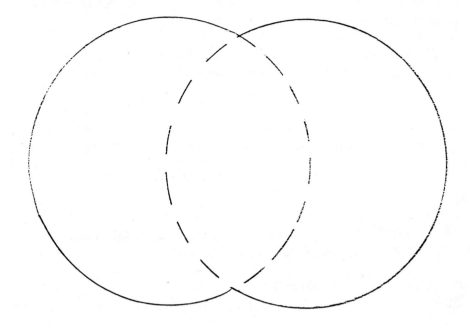

Sketch of name substitute   Sketch of visually enhanced
                                   physical characteristic

(The combined sketches also should "ring your bell," giving you an association when you need it.)

To summarize:

- A word which represents a concrete image substitute for a person's name is called a <u>picture word.</u>

- An image or a picture which represents a picture word is called a <u>word picture</u>.

- A visually enhanced image of a person's outstanding physical characteristic is called a <u>fantasy image</u>.

- A name substitute sketch connected to a fantasy image sketch associates the person's name with the outstanding feature. These completed sketches are called <u>ringers</u>.

Here is how I would organize the steps to obtain a ringer.

NAME	FACE
ACTION:	ACTION:

1. GET THE NAME DOWN

1. DETERMINE OUTSTANDING FEATURE

2. NAME ENHANCEMENT

2. VISUAL ENHANCEMENT

RHYMERS	BIZARRE
SYNONYMS	EXAGGERATION
MATCHING PAIRS	ACTION

=   =

PICTURE WORD NAME SUBSTITUTE   FANTASY IMAGE

\   /

FORM THE RINGER

RHYMERS

Let's provide you with more experience composing and sketching picture words. On a sheet of paper see if you can write picture words for each of the following surnames. You'll find that soundalikes are the easiest to derive. (We can't sketch the fantasy images and the ringers because we don't know what these people look like.)

It's not an easy exercise. The list contains a liberal sprinkling of frequently found Asian and Latin names, as I pulled them out of a Los Angeles phone book. Skip to those you can do quickly. Fill in the others over time as you become better at it.

I have started you out by listing picture words which seem to go with the names of the first six.   My completed list of picture words can be found in Appendix C.

Abalos   - abalone, Appaloosa, Apollos

Abbott   - a butt

Abdullah   - a dull H

Abell   - A bell; ape ball

Abernathy   - a natty bear

Abraham   - a brown ham

Abrams   -

Abrego   -

Acevedo   -

Aceves   -

Ackerman   -

Acosta   -

Adame   -

Addison   -

Adkins   -

Agopian   -

Aguilar   -

Aiken   -

Akopyan   -

Alarcon   -

Alas   -

Alba   -

Albert   -

Alcala   -

Alcantara   -

Alcaraz   -

Aldana   -

Alejo   -

Aleman   -

Alex   -

Alfaro   -

Alfonso   -

Alford   -

Allen   -

Allison   -

Alonso   -

Alpert   -

Alston   -

Altman   -

Alvarado   -

If you had difficulty finding rhymers, your computer can assist you. Go to Utilities. Highlight each name for which you need a rhymer and spell check it. In many cases, you'll need to break the name into syllables, and then spell check the syllables.

You can go through the same process with the thesaurus in your word processing program to find synonyms.

If you don't have a computer, you always can open the dictionary and your thesaurus book. But, the fun is finding good associating words from your own brain cells.

PHRASE LINKS

Now let's try to form memorable name substitutes using phrase links. Here are some easy English first names. My answers are in Appendix C.

Beth   - Matt (Bath mat)

Bobbie   - Sox (Bobby sox)

Chester   - Drawers (Chest of drawers)

Doris

Earl

Eugene

Frank

Gerrie

Grant

Harold

Helen

Howard

Jack

Karen

Lane

Philip

Robin

Roland

Ryan

Ruth

Sam

Selma

Susan

Wallace

Here's another list of first names. Specialize the phrase links by adding a famous person's last name. If you remember the famous person when you meet your acquaintance, you will recall the acquaintance's first name.

Alan   - Greenspan

Dwight   - Eisenhower

Emerson   - Fitipaldi

Eva

Evander

Fidel

George

Gloria

Imelda

Leonardo

Maria

Mario

Michael

Noel

Olympia

Paula

Rene

Richard

Rush

Salvador

Sylvia

Teresa

Woody

Practice, practice, practice.

You might want to start a separate <u>PICTURE-WORD FILE</u>. Keep adding names and their picture words. When you have a thick file, you'll be able to look up the names of many new acquaintances and attach a picture word substitute for each name right from your Picture Word File.

Unlike when recording information in your Meetings Notebook, using a card file or a Rolodex file works very nicely for picture words because you can file the names alphabetically. It's also easy if you use a computer, which allows you to insert and sort names alphabetically without rewriting.

Okay. You've written down the names of the people you met at the meeting and sketched substitutes for their names. You then sketched fantasy images of their prominent features in an enhanced form and tied the two sketches together for each person, forming ringers. You are tired. Go to bed.

REFRESHMENT TIME

The morning after the meeting, refresh your memory using your Meetings Notebook. Visualize the people in the room. Note the outstanding features you sketched for those you met and the ringers you formed. Repeat aloud each name. By picturing everyone back in the room where you met them, you should, upon a chance meeting with a Ruth Katchen again, be able to remember not only her name, but the circumstances under which you first met.

A QUESTION?

How are you supposed to remember a person's background? I never touched upon that. Well, I didn't want to give it all to you at once.

It would be helpful, in addition to remembering peoples' names and where you met, if you could recall something about who they are and their interests.

Just a little more sketching, please.

For example: If Bob Cook is a bus driver, let's just enclose our sketch of him inside a bus. If he is a lawyer we can draw a stick arm holding the scales of justice. If he is a tennis pro, put a racquet in his hand.

Not too difficult.

Time for a coffee break.

CHAPTER FOUR

ADDITIONAL AIDS FOR REMEMBERING NAMES

My computer can probably render
A universe lacking in gender.
The point of creation
In this simulation
Is something I fail to remember.

I concede my computer now knows
More each day, for its memory grows.
But I still can't explain
How a silicon brain
Can know that I know that it knows!

Playboy, March 1977

THE TWELVE AMAZING STEPS

Let's review the process. Here are the <u>Twelve Amazing Steps to Names and Faces Glory</u>.

1. Tell yourself again you have the desire to become the monarch of memory.

2. Demonstrate your intent to remember names and faces by noting it next to each meeting and party listed on your calendar.

3. Buy a notebook and label it Meetings Notebook. Put it in your briefcase or car.

4. Do not give your name to any strangers before you hear their names, have the names spelled, and you repeat them from two to five times.

5. Learn about the background, personality and occupation of the people you meet. Make them do the talking.

6. Observe each face, mentally checking off features from the chart of outstanding features. Determine which feature is the most distinctive. If you are able to at that time, exaggerate in bizarre fashion that feature.

7. Observe those you have met from a distance, noting their physical characteristics, posture, attitude, and mannerisms. Get side views of their faces.

8. As soon as you leave the event, write in your Meetings Notebook the date, name of the event, it's purpose and where it was held. Visualize the event. Write the names, outstanding characteristics and background information of the people you met. List their outstanding features and describe them or draw them in the visually enhanced form.

9. Before you go to sleep complete the ringers. Coin and visualize a substitute for each person's name that is not already an image and sketch it next to the fantasy image sketch of the most striking feature. Add to the sketches something to remind you of their occupations or their interests.

10. In the morning, review the names, information and sketches.

11. Add each name substitute to your Picture Word File.

12. Once a week, refresh your memory.

(My wife says I am too structured. I don't think so. Do you?)

Now you have all the tools for remembering names and faces.

SHORTCUTS

I'm here to make your life easier.

You want to go to a meeting and come away with more than just a few names in your memory. You don't want to become overwhelmed with the task of remembering a bucketful of names so that you don't get anything else out of the meeting.

Why not commit the names to memory before the meeting?

That's right - before the meeting.

Usually, there is an invitation list. Obtain it and memorize the list beforehand. Since you'll have all the names, you can write out your list of picture words in advance. Save you a lot of work.

Even though you might not be a member, some organizations will mail out their membership directory, if requested, especially if you indicate that you are attending one of their meetings. It might cost a few dollars, but it could be very worthwhile. The directories usually will list the officers, and the officers often will be in attendance at the meeting.

Every year I used to go to the Sundance Film festival in Park City, Utah. The festival sponsors printed advance sheets with the names of the registrants, their companies and in which hotels they were staying. Since I was trying to sell my screenplays, I was interested in meeting all the agents, directors and producers in attendance.

I wrote down and drew picture words for each person I wanted to meet. I also envisioned them in the hotel where they were staying. When I met one, it was a snap to mentally attach the picture word to his prominent feature. When I asked him how he liked his hotel, he was impressed that I knew where he was staying. You can bet each time I ran into him during the week's festivities, I called him by name.

Too bad all that good work didn't help me sell my screenplays. But I can't blame it on my memory.

TABLE HOPPING

Now you say you can't get advance sheets for your meetings, so what I just told you is a waste of time. Don't tell me there won't be any name badges, either. Or names on tent cards on the tables.

There's always a way to get the names. If you want to be very good at this, get to the meeting early. Give yourself time to look over the names. Carry a small notebook. Write the names, table by table. Wow! If you have all the names, table by table, see how much easier it will be for you to make your entries in the Meetings Notebook after the meeting.

Obtaining the names in advance is not limited to meetings or parties.

When I practiced law, it was great to be able to address a jury and call each juror by his name without any notes. It sure impressed the jurors. How did I do this? - simple. I obtained the list of potential jurors in advance from the court clerk. I made picture words for their names. When the jurors were called to sit in the jury box, I merely attached the picture word to their outstanding features, and I was home free.

If you can't remember all the enhancements you visualized for the faces or all the names of the people you met until you get outside and can draw your ringers in your Meetings Notebook, write them on a small note pad during the meeting.

For those few of you who find my method of remembering names and faces too difficult, there still is the plain old English Alphabet. If you cannot remember a name, picture that person in your mind as you repeat aloud the letters of the English Alphabet. More often than you think, you will stop at the first letter of the name of that person, and it will cause the full name to pop into your head. Sometimes I can get the first letter, but still not the name. I follow with adding a vowel as the second letter, and frequently I then get the pop.

Finally - your future. From middle age on, names become harder to remember. It becomes even more important to refresh your memory by repeating the names of people you want to remember.

If you pause to remember your spouse's name, I can tell you, you are in deep trouble.

CHAPTER FIVE

THE NUMERICAL ORDER ALPHABET

An elderly couple, Sadie and Sam were in their bedroom when Sadie asked Sam to go to the kitchen for her. "Write it down," she said, "so you won't forget this time. I want a slice of apple pie. Heat some caramel and spread it on. Then add a spoonful of vanilla ice cream." As Sam started off with his note, she called out, "And add a cherry on top." When Sam came back, he carried in only a hot dog on a plate. And Sadie said, "And where's the mustard?"

The Hook Method is the technique we will learn for establishing short-term relationships between names, objects or concepts and a number of permanently-remembered key picture words (an alphabet). Before you can start hooking (Chapter Six), you'll need to acquire an alphabet.

The Numerical Order Alphabet was one of the first cue systems devised. Cue systems are tools of association which can be utilized for recall. The Numerical Order Alphabet consists of a series of key picture words. You will memorize this alphabet and refresh it frequently so that it remains in your conscious mind forever.

The Numerical Order Alphabet will be useful whenever you want to recall lists of items in their particular order of succession. Because the concept is so important to understand, let me paraphrase by stating that when you wish to recall a list of items in their proper sequence, the Numerical Order Alphabet is the best tool to use.

Later, we will learn other alphabets, but none of them can transpose picture words directly into numbers. They are useful when we don't need to know the order of the items.

The Numerical Order Alphabet is used in one form or another by most mnemonists.

A LITTLE HISTORY

A. S. Boyd in his book "The World's Important Facts and How to Remember Them," 5th Edition, 1886, mentions that in 1846, Professor Pliny Miles delivered lectures which described the Numerical Order Alphabet. It originally consisted of 100 picture words which converted to numbers. I call this the primary Numerical Order Alphabet, to which I have added a secondary list of 100 picture words, bringing the total to 200.

You might be impressed to think that the Numerical Order Alphabet goes back to 1846, but wait. Stanislaus Mink von Wennsshein introduced the concept around 1648. Dr. Richard Grey expanded on it in 1730. It has been revised and re-worked many times since then.

YOU CAN USE ALL TEN FINGERS

Here are the first ten key words of the primary Numerical Order Alphabet. Each word will represent forever the number it follows.

1. Tea

2. Noah

3. May

4. Ray

5. Law

6. Jaw

7. Key

8. Fee

9. Bay

10. Toes

Notice how May and Ray rhyme, as well as Law and Jaw; Key and Fee. It makes memorizing and using them so much easier.

For starters, read the list aloud three times and write the numbers and the key words as you do so. Three times probably will not impress them sufficiently in your memory for later full recall, but it's a good start.

Do it now.

I promised my six-year-old grandson a dollar when he could memorize the first ten. I had to pay off within one day! A little incentive goes a long way.

Did you earn the dollar?

I'LL GIVE YOU A CUE

How was tea chosen to represent a 1? How were the other nine particular words chosen? Good questions.

Of course, there are reasons.

The Numerical Order Alphabet is a phonetic alphabet which relies on the sounds of speech. Since the words in the alphabet will be transposed to numbers, we need a Transposing Code in which certain letters of the English Alphabet will represent the digits from zero to nine.

In our Transposing Code - as shown in the diagram on the next page - any number which begins with the digit 1 will always be associated with the letters d, t and th. The digit 2 will be associated with the letter n. The digit 3 goes with m. The digit 4 with r. 5 with l. 6 with the sound of sh, j, ch or a soft g. 7 with k, q, a hard g, or c, and with ng. 8 with f, ph or v. 9 with b and p. Zero with s, z and a soft c.

The reverse, letters to numbers, have the same relationships.

So when tea was chosen to represent a 1, it was because the t in tea always will be associated with the digit 1. Noah has an n, so it will represent the digit 2. And so on.

The number 10 is different. It has two digits. Toes was chosen since it has a t for the digit 1 and an s for the digit 0.

Since the Numerical Order Alphabet is a consonant-based alphabet, we ignore the vowels.

A diagram of the Transposing Code looks like this:

0	1	2	3	4	5	6	7	8	9
s	t	n	m	r	l	sh	k	f	b
z	th					ch	q	v	p
soft c	d					j	ng	ph	
					soft g	hard g			
					hard c				

Again, vowels are not part of this alphabet. Neither are the consonants w, h or y, which are considered to be vowels unless they are attached to a letter to make a sound (as in SH or CH). ["WHY" for memory retention].

Since it is the sound of the consonant which is important in the Numerical Order Alphabet, when you translate words to numbers or numbers to words, you should articulate the words so as to know the sounds the letters make in the words. Silent letters, such as the K in knowledge, are omitted.

I'll give you two examples of how a consonant might represent two separate digits:

1) Each g in garage is pronounced differently and is treated differently by the Numerical Order Alphabet. The first g is hard, while the second g is soft. According to the Transposing Code diagram, when we translate these letters into numbers, the first will represent a 7 and the latter will represent a 6.

2) Similarly, the first c in circus is soft, representing a zero, while the latter is hard, representing a 7.

g a r a g e   c i r c u s

7   4   6   0   47   0

See, nothing to it.

It is essential you commit to memory, right now, the letter sounds representing the digits from 0 to 9.

You should get to know them just like you know your ABCs. From this day forth, you will be referring to the letters of the Numerical Order Alphabet much more often than you will your ABCs.

For practice, whenever you see a number such as a telephone number, your check number or the number on a license plate, translate the number into its letter sounds, and do it aloud.

You should be able to read 5826 as l,f,n,ch.   Alternately, you could read it as l,v,n,sh or l,v,n,j.

If you see the number 141, you should be able to read it as t,r,t. You also can use a d or a th to represent the number 1. Then you should be able to convert the number 141 into a word such as: dart, dirt, tardy, third, trade, tried, thirty, tirade, trout or trot.

Also develop the habit of translating words to numbers.

If you hear a person's name, think of it as a number. Marilyn is 3452. Do it with any words. Globe is 759. Amazing is 307.

PRACTICE, PRACTICE, PRACTICE

Here's a little practice:

Translate the following words to numbers and the numbers to words. Use a sheet of paper.

Fortunate	_____	93 _____
Typewriter	_____	57 _____
Helen	_____	44 _____
Computer	_____	61 _____
Panasonic	_____	129 _____
Concise	_____	152 _____
Mark	_____	4344 _____
Wedding	_____	9573 _____

You thought it was easy didn't you, until you reached 129? And even harder with 4344. Hey, I don't give easy tests. I want to stretch your mind.

Don't get upset if you couldn't think of words that translate into three and four digit numbers. I'll make it easy for you - later in the game.

SEE IT INSIDE YOUR HEAD

The next step in your education is to visualize the first ten key words of the Numerical Order Alphabet. This is achieved best by utilizing familiar mental images of the items the words represent, but in forms which are different from the norm. This is where imagination really comes into play.

I am thankful now for all the fairy tales I read as a kid. For several summers, I read three of them every day. They put a paper fish in the fishbowl at the Lima, Ohio public library for each one I read. I was very proud of that.

I owe my imagination and my ability to visualize to my early experience with those fairy-tale books. It was a skill developed by interest. Even if you don't have a skilled imagination, it is never too late to develop it.

WE GOT THE TOOLS

First, let's think about how the pictures should look. Here's another chance to use various enhancement methods (from Chapter Two).

To picture Tea, the word which represents the number 1 in the Numerical Order Alphabet, we could imagine a tea bag in cup of tea so large that the cup sits on the floor. The cup could be a bright red. Doing that, we have exaggerated size and color. What if the cup were tipped so that tea were spilling out - [Action Method].

For the number 2, we could have Noah standing on a bright yellow ark. What if there were more than one Noah? - [Multiplication Method]. What if waves were washing up? - [Action Method].

For the number 3, let's visualize a very large calendar page with the month of May imprinted on it. We have transformed the concept of a month to an object.

For Ray, let's envisage a futuristic ray gun.

For <u>Law</u>, a lady policeman standing in the middle of an intersection holding up a huge hand to stop traffic while the other hand holds a giant policeman's badge.

For <u>Jaw</u>, perhaps a large protruding mandible. Could stick a cigar in the mouth for special effect. Better yet, we could substitute a flower or a toilet plunger. Easier to remember? You might even substitute the jaw of the great white shark from the movie "Jaws."

For <u>Key</u>, a large key. Perhaps the color green to make it different from any ordinary key. For those of you who remember skeleton keys, you might picture the shape of one of them. What if it were lying on a table, nearly falling off?

For <u>Fee</u>, picture a midget clerk behind a barred window at a counter accepting your fine for parking violations.

For <u>Bay</u>, a raft floating on a large body of water surrounded by mountains. What if the bay were red? We could dream up a shark fin circling a raft loaded with bathing beauties.

Since the number 10 has two consonants, it requires a t and an s - <u>Toes</u>. Picture a foot with only three very large toes.

Putting it all together, by verbalizing [expressing numbers in a certain order and assigning picture words to each] and by visualizing [mentally picturing the words as unusual and distinguishable objects - word pictures] we have a list of ten key words that make up the beginning of the Numerical Order Alphabet.

I went into a number of computer image programs seeking objects to represent these numbers as word pictures. Of course, none of the programs have the kind of bizarre or zany images that we seek. But for most of the numbers from one to one hundred I found representations of our picture words. Based on these somewhat ordinary pictures, you can let your imaginations run rampant as you form your own visualizations for the Numerical Order Alphabet.

You can find these first ten word pictures in Appendix F - Illustration One. Just look at the first ten word pictures for now. We'll get to the others later.

Note that most of the key words utilize the vowel a or e. As we move ahead to give key words for the numbers 11 through 100, you will observe the same general pattern. Perhaps you've guessed why it's done this way. In case you haven't, I'll reveal the secret.

Suppose you need to remember all your Numerical Order Alphabet key words, but you can't recall the key word for the number 7. You know 7 always is a k or a hard g or c. So start with the hard sound of k and the vowel a - no familiar visual object pops up. Then try k with the vowel e - oh, it's <u>Key</u>.

Occasionally, after you have mastered the list of the first 100 key words of the Numerical Order Alphabet, you will fail momentarily to remember one of the words on the list. To recall it, you might have to go through the vowels to o or even to u to recall the dropped key word. To make the system work fastest, we try to use memorable key words which have an a as the first vowel, since it is the first vowel we will test each time with our consonant.

If we can't design a word that fits when using an a, we search for good picture words which have an e. If a, e, i, o or u don't work, we can use combinations of vowels. Simple, isn't it?

With the number 2, following words have the sound of an n as the only pronounced consonant (excluding the sounds of h, w and y):

No, now, Noah, an, anew, annoy, any, hen, honey, in, inn, neigh, win, wine, when, own, hyena.

Out of this list, Noah was the best picture word which the originator of the Primary Numerical Order Alphabet could visualize mentally, even though he had to use the combination of o and a. Although a hen makes a good mental picture, it is harder to remember a word when the consonant comes after a vowel or one of the three non-used consonants in "why".

Before proceeding to learning how to use the Numerical Order Alphabet as a cue system, you need to fix the first ten key words in your memory.

TIME FOR YOU TO GET TO WORK

Get comfortable. Lock the door. Turn off any extraneous sounds or other distractions. Be ready to concentrate. Avoid interference and displacement.

Read aloud and write the numbers and key words. As you recite each, visualize the pictures as I have above drawn them. If you want to change any picture to one more readily visualized by you, it's okay.

When you think you have the pictures in mind and the list memorized, test yourself. Randomly translate the numbers to words and the words to numbers. Be able to do it almost without thinking.

It's a kick!

Are you sure you have the alphabet solid? Good.

Just because you have it solidly in your mind now, it doesn't mean you will have it there tomorrow.

You can bank the Numerical Order Alphabet into your long-term memory just as you learned the English Alphabet - by daily repetition. But because the first letter of each of the key words has a relationship to one of the numbers, it should be faster.

Every morning before you get out of bed, repeat the list. If you need an external aid, paste the list to your bathroom mirror or the refrigerator. After the alphabet has been installed in your long-term memory, a once a week refresher should be enough to maintain it against fading.

REFRESHMENT TIME

Throughout the first part of this book, you saw that important concepts were underlined. As a way of better recalling them, you could have summarized and outlined them in written notes. Because these concepts are the foundation for the rest of the book, I have done this job for you this one time. Don't read on to more of the good stuff until you really know these concepts. I may test you on them later on.

GLOSSARY OF CONCEPTS AND TERMS

Memory   - Past observations and concepts capable of
                             being recalled into your conscious mind.

Immediate, Working or Ultra Short-Term Memory -

                             Materials that can be reproduced within a span of attention,
                             but will be lost in seconds or minutes.

Recent or Short-Term Memory -

                             Where you have the ability to acquire and
                             retain new information and can repeat the
                             material after a brief delay.

Remote, Permanent or Long-term Memory -

                             Where you can retrieve information learned in
                             the distant past.

Semantic Memory -

>   The general knowledge you have stored up
>   over the years.

Episodic Memory -

>   That memory which is personal to you, such as what
>   movies you have seen, what you had to eat yesterday, who
>   you dated

Implicit Memory -

>   Deals with body functions, especially motor skills.

Encoding   - A method of modifying of information so that
                       it can be placed in memory. Also called
                       registering.

Observation   - The seeing, hearing or feeling with interest.

Retention   - The maintenance within the brain of observed
                       material that is capable of being retrieved
                       into the conscious mind.

Recall   - The retrieval from the subconscious mind of
                       stored information.

Displacement   - The replacing of something in your memory by
                       something else.

Fading   - The gradual loss of memories so that they
                       become inaccessible.

Expansion   - The filling in of gaps in our memory by the
                       subconscious mind.

Reconstruction   - The addition of details to a memory each time
                       it is recalled.

Interference   - Any sensory input other than from the
                       absorption of the desired material.

Memory systems   - Artificial methods of enhancing memory.

Cue systems   - Methods of association that can be utilized
                       for recall, the most common of which is the
                       Numerical Order Alphabet.

Repetition - The use of any of the senses to "observe" an item or concept more than once.

Organization - The process of summarizing, outlining and classifying information.

Summarization - The making of a brief statement about the content of a topic.

Outlining - The listing of the important points of a number of topics.

Classification - The grouping together of like material.

Association - The relating of two or more things to each other, at least one of which is present in your conscious mind.

Enhancement - Methods of association by which the object, idea or thing to be remembered is made more prominent than others less important, such as by the use of multiplication and zany poses.

Picture words - Words that can be represented by images.

Word pictures - Images which represent words.

Fantasy image - A visually enhanced image of a person's outstanding physical characteristic.

Ringers - The connecting of fantasy image sketches of outstanding physical features with word pictures of name substitutes.

Transposing Code -

The code where certain consonants of the English Alphabet represent the digits from zero to nine.

Key Words - Words that instantly cause us to recall something to which they are associated.

Acronyms - Words formed from the first letters or syllables of other words.

Acrostics　　　　　- Arrangements of words in which the first or
　　　　　　　　　　　last letter in each line, taken in order,
　　　　　　　　　　　spell a phrase.

CHAPTER SIX

THE HOOK METHOD

A patient came in to see me because of his
loss of memory. I made him pay in advance.

You now will learn how to remember lists of unrelated items through the use of the Hook Method, by which you will visually attach or hook unrelated things, events, and concepts to the picture words of the Numerical Order Alphabet. With the Hook Method, you not only will be able to remember all the items on a list, but you will remember the order or sequence of each item.

The process of association is an integral part of the Hook Method. Again, association is the connecting of new information with something you already know.

What do you know? You know the first ten picture words of the Numerical Order Alphabet. Before you finish reading this book, you will know the first 200 picture words of the Numerical Order Alphabet. You will be repeating this basic alphabet daily (until it is firmly memorized), and then weekly (to refresh). Your intention will be to remember this alphabet the rest of your life because you are motivated to have a better memory.

Each word in the Numerical Order Alphabet is the picture hook on which you will mentally hang the material you want to remember.

HERE THEY ARE AGAIN

Following is the group of ten objects which you attempted to remember at the beginning of Chapter Two.

Computer

Bagpipes

Suitcase

Thermometer

Carpet

Oak tree

Rainbow

Elephant

Fire hydrant

Garden hose

Now, when you want to remember this collection of items, and in their proper sequence, you will use Hook Method - by which you will associate the items with the key words of the Numerical Order Alphabet.

How are you going to remember "computer?" Since it is the first object on the list, you will want to visualize the picture words for the number 1. Remember, it is a huge red teacup and tea bag representing the word tea. Now make an association between the teacup and the computer by hooking them together. Why not have the tea cup setting on top of a computer? To make the picture more memorable, have the cup overflowing and the tea dripping down on the keyboard in violation of the rule of never eating or drinking near a computer keyboard. You have utilized the enhancement methods of action and bizarre exaggeration to make the picture so unusual, it will stick in your memory.

When you want to recall the list, you will visualize the word picture for the number 1. As soon as you see the tea cup, you immediately will associate it with the computer.

The reverse is equally applicable. If you know all the items on the list, but wish to recall their sequence, just visualize the computer. You immediately will see the dripping teacup on top of it and know that it was the first on the list.

To remember the second item - bagpipes - you might visualize Noah on the arc playing a bagpipe while the animals dance to the music.

For the third item - suitcase - imagine that the photo at the top of the May calendar is of huge, odd-shaped suitcases. Give them vivid colors and paste all kinds of travel labels on them. Maybe name tags with the name "Dr. May."

For item number four - thermometer - envision a thermometer sticking out of the red hot ray. You could have the mercury bubbling out of the top of the thermometer.

For the fifth item - carpet - think of a fat policewoman standing on a magic carpet that hovers over the street. She is wobbling as she tries to maintain her balance.

For the sixth item - oak tree - see a clown hanging from an oak tree by his jaw.

For the seventh item - rainbow - envision a key sticking out of the pot of gold at the base of a rainbow. Gold coins are overflowing the pot.

For the eighth item - elephant - imagine paying an admission fee to see an elephant on display. The elephant is balancing himself on a large ball.

For item number nine - fire hydrant - a huge fire hydrant is filling up the bay.

For the tenth item - garden hose - the toes are dancing on the garden hose.

Got the idea?

When making your associations, you can put objects on top of each other, below each other or inside each other. You can place them in ridiculous situations and color them abnormally. You can make substitutions and put them in unusual positions or places. There is no limit on the number or types of associations you can make.

If you can, give them a sound, a smell, a taste and a touch. The addition of each sense makes the object and the association more memorable.

HERE COMES THE TEST

Review the list of ten items one more time, visualizing the associations. When you close the book, count to ten. As you count each number, visualize the key word and the item hooked to it. Then do the reverse. Picture the item and determine its sequence.

I'll go get a bite to eat.

Close the book.

Are you back? Good. I'll bet you remembered all of them. Or at least nine out of the ten. And that's just for starters. Every day, have one of your friends or associates give you a new list. You'll find that the items from the previous day will be easily displaced by the new list. Soon, you'll be ready to work with larger groups of items, and you will be using all 100 key words from the primary Numerical Order Alphabet. That comes with Chapter Seven.

But let's start with 30, and I'll add the rest later on. I'll even provide you with the secondary set of 100 key words.

I know your next question - "Do you really have 200 key words in your permanent memory which you can instantly transpose from all the numbers from 1 to 200?" Of course, I do. I learned them through concentration and perseverance, through verbalization and visualization. You are going to do this, too, because you are motivated ... and you don't want to have wasted your time or money.

This time I will allow you to make up your own word pictures. In the space next to each number draw how you would visualize the word picture for it. Remember, the more bizarre or zany, the better you will remember it. You can amplify it, multiply it and add action to it.

Later, you may want to go back and add color to the picture. Since you will keep this book for many years, you might want to draw your word pictures on a sheet of paper first, and then come back later and enter them into this book. [Basic sample word pictures for the numbers 11 to 30 are shown in Appendix F - Illustration Two.]

Here goes.

11. has the sound of t or d twice.

The key word is <u>Tot</u>. I picture a

fat tot busting through a playpen.

12. has the sound of a t or d and

an n. The key word is <u>Tan</u>. I picture

bathing beauties on a beach getting tans.

Or how about a can of tan shoe polish?

13. has the sound of a t or a d plus an m. The key word is <u>Tam</u>. I picture a huge orange top hat. (I know "tam" is outdated, but, remember, the primary alphabet was devised in the 1800s.)

14. has the sound of a t or a d plus an r. The key word is <u>Tar</u>, and I envision a pool of tar leaking out of a very large barrel.

15. has the sound of a t or a d plus an l. I see a rattlesnake's <u>Tail</u>.

16. has the sound of a t or a d plus a ch or an sh. I see a Kleenex <u>Tissue</u> box.

17. has a second sound of a k. It's a <u>Tack</u>.

18. has a second sound of an f or a ph. It's <u>Taffy</u>.

19. has a second sound of a b

or a p. It's beer keg <u>Tap</u>. (You

also could visualize a water tap.)

You know how to do the next ten. They all start with the letter n since n is a 2 in the Numerical Order Alphabet.

20.   Nose - how about

Pinocchio's nose?

21. Net - a fisherman's net

or a butterfly net.

22. Noon - picture the sun

at high noon.

23. Name - envision your

name inscribed on a desk plaque.

24. Nero - he's holding a
fiddle.

25. Nail - a spike.

26. Niche - visualize a niche
in a wall.

27. Neck - see a giraffe's neck.

28. Navy - picture a battleship.

29. Nap - a sleeping peasant with
a large sombrero.

PICTURE TIME

Time to start committing this list to memory. Make your visual pictures of each key word (the "Word Pictures") as you organize the words according to their number and sounds. It's going to be easier than you anticipate. You might want to prepare a set of flash cards.

Soon, you will learn how to remember numbers containing more than two digits. But in each case, the Numerical Order Alphabet is applied. Thus <u>Mustang</u> would represent 3017.

A FEW SPECIAL RULES

In his book "Assimilative Memory or How to Attend and Never Forget," 1896, Professor A. Loisette enumerated some special rules of the Numerical Order Alphabet:

1. Two consonants of the same kind with no vowel between, provided they have the same sound, are treated as one consonant, as ll = 5, nn = 2, rr = 4, dd = 1, etc. The first two consonants have different values in the word "accident" = 70121.

2. All silent consonants are disregarded, as b in "lamb" = 53, "comb" = 73, or in "tomb" = 13. The g is disregarded in "bought" = 91 and in "neighbors" = 2940; the k in "know" = 2; the l in "could" = 71.

3. Combinations of consonants have the same value as their soundalikes, as gh in "tough" = 18 and the gh in "enough" = 28 because the gh sounds like an f. "Phrase" = 840. With "lock" it = 57 because the ck sounds just like a k.

You might wonder why I used only a t in the second ten key words and not one d. It's because I saved the d to use for the key words for 111 - 119 or in a second list of 1 - 100. It makes it easier to alternate lists if I use them frequently and there is not enough time for displacement to occur. All the key words are organized wherever possible for ease of recall and to avoid confusion,.

Now that you are well on your way to having 30 hooks - keep repeating and visualizing them.

THE HOOK METHOD IN PRACTICAL USE

What if you are taking a course in early American history and you are to be tested on the evolution of the rifle? You'll need to remember the name of each rifle and the order in which it was used. Let's try using the Hook Method.

After the name of each rifle, we will picture one of the key picture words you have learned.

1. The Springfield rifle. A cup of Tea stands on a huge spring and swings back and forth.

2. The Cartridge rifle. Noah tossing carts off of the arc onto a ridge.

3. Small Game rifles. A miniature checker board lying on the month of May of a calendar.

4. The Colt rifles. A Ray of light on a young horse.

5. The Sharps rifle. A Law man holding a large pointed sharp knife.

6. The Winchester rifle. A Jaw lying in an open chest.

7. The Remington rifle. A Key inserted into a Remington shaver or an old Remington typewriter.

8. The Savage rifle. A headhunter paying a traffic Fee.

9. The Stevens rifle. Steven Spielberg loading a ship in the Bay.

10. The Ballard rifle. Toes wrapped around a ball in a yard. (You might want to visualize toes in ballet slippers).

11. The Marlin rifle. A Tot shooting at a Marlin.

12. The Iver Johnson rifle. A shoe shine boy with a can of Tan polish in front of an ivy covered Howard Johnson's Motel.

13. The Newton rifle. A Tam filled to the brim with Fig Newtons on top of Sir Isaac Newton's head.

14. The Mossberg rifle. Moss on an iceberg floating on hot Tar.

15. The Johnson automatic rifles. Former President Johnson waving a rolled Tale parchment at a crowd.

16. The Garand rifle. A box of Tissue and a rifle inside a garland of flowers.

Garand is not in the dictionary. I had to find a good rhymer or soundalike. Garland is as close as I could get, and a wreath of flowers or leaves is easily visualized and offbeat enough to be memorable.

In the process of memorizing rifles we saw that since names may not be easily recalled, it was important to transpose the name into an object. The same applies to concepts.

For example: If a speaker plans to include the subject of gravity in his talk about the forces in nature, and he wants to use a memory method, he can transpose the concept of gravity into something which can be visualized. Since Newton watched an apple fall when he discovered gravity, the speaker might use an apple to represent the concept of gravity.

TEST TIME

Yes, the test. If you think I'm going to let you get away without making sure you know the stuff I spent so much time preparing for you, you're wrong. I'm not doing this for my health. So let's get on with the test.

I gave you the first 29 key words of the Numerical Order Alphabet. You practiced the first ten key words on the group of unrelated objects from Chapter Two. You have now just completed picturing the first sixteen key words on the list of rifles. The following is a list of the first 29 numbers. Write down the key word for each.

You should have the first sixteen key words well in mind, and I would accept correct answers to at least eleven of the next thirteen. If you don't score a total of at least 27 out of the 29, do not pass GO. Do not start the next chapter.

STOP! I didn't say write the words in this sacred book. Get a sheet of paper and write down the numbers from 1 to 29 on it.

1.   16.

2.   17.

3.   18.

4.   19.

5.   20.

6.   21.

7.   22.

8.   23.

9.   24.

10.   25.

11.   26.

12.   27.

13.   28.

14.   29.

15.

The Hook Method can be used for more than just taking tests. You can use it to remember telephone numbers, addresses, appointments, errands, shopping lists, birthdays, dates, statistics, and more. We'll cover some of these in later chapters.

DISTINGUISHING FEATURES OF THE NUMERICAL ORDER ALPHABET

It is important to know when the Numerical Order Alphabet is best applied.

1. Use of the Numerical Order Alphabet is primarily for the retention of material in our short-term memory, because each time we use the key words in association with new material the older associations will be displaced.

Because of displacement, I have developed other alphabet cue systems. They are the Animals Alphabet, the Body Parts Alphabet, the Days of the Week Alphabet, the Months Alphabet, the Dressing Alphabet, your Home Street Alphabet, your Home Town Alphabet, your House Alphabet, and the Time Alphabet.

By using these additional alphabets in rotation, you can keep separate lists in memory for longer periods, since the same key words need not be used as often. They will be described in Chapters Ten, Twelve, Thirteen and Fourteen.

2. The Numerical Order Alphabet is the best alphabet to use when it is important to know the sequence or numerical order of each item on the list, because the picture words transpose directly into numbers.

Remember that night in Algiers
When we polished off three dozen beers
And all eight ugly broads
At Fatima & __
How our memories fade with the years.

Martin Wellborn

CHAPTER SEVEN

THE COMPLETE NUMERICAL ORDER ALPHABET

Three things happen when you get older.
One you lose your memory and...uh...I
forgot the other two.

It's time to give you the picture words for the numbers from 30 to 100 in the primary Numerical Order Alphabet, and for you to draw the word pictures. I'll give you the basic idea - you amplify it with zaniness, action, multiplication and color. Basic images culled from clip art are included in Appendix F - Illustration Three for your reference. They need your personal embellishment.

30. Mass - a priest holding

mass or a choir in a church.

31. Mat - a mat outside your

front door.

32. Man - how about a snow man?

33. Mama - a mother wheeling a baby carriage.

34. Mare - could be a horse jumping a fence or a rocking horse.

35. Mail - the mail box next to the street.

36. Match - an open pack of matches.

37. Mic - a microphone.

38. Muff - a girl with her hands in a muff.

39. Map - a map of your state.

40. Race - two hurdlers running next to each other or an Indy 500 race.

41. Rat - a very big one snarling at you.

42. Rain - a person under a multi-colored umbrella in a downpour.

43. Ram - a ram on a mountain peak.

44. Rear - the back door of your house.

45. Rail - a set of train rails.

46. Rash - a poison ivy rash on your arm.

47. Rake - a rake leaning against your house.

48. Reef - a South Pacific reef
with a few palm trees on it.

49. Rope - a coil of rope.

50. Lace - a lace table cloth.

51. Lot - how about a monstrous
grasshopper in a lot next to a house.

52. Lane - a road bordered by
rows of trees.

53. Lime - a pile of large green limes on a table.

54. Lair - a rabbit peering out of its lair.

55. Lily - a beautiful white lily in a vase.

56. Lash - a whip.

57. Lake - a lake filled with boats and surrounded by mountains.

58. Leaf - a very large oak leaf.

59. Lap - a woman holding a big salad bowl in her lap or a laptop computer.

60. Chase - a man chasing a woman and being chased himself by a woman.

61. Chat - two people chatting.

62. Chain - a large anchor chain.

63. Chime - a set of bells chiming.

64. Chair - a director's chair.

65. Chile - Chile on a map of
South America.

66. Judge - he's banging a huge
gavel.

67. Check - a large check mark.

68. Chef - a smiling cook wearing
a large chef's hat.

69. Chip - a pile of wood chips.

70. Case - a briefcase.

71. Cat - it's large and its hair is standing straight on end.

72. Can - a green paint can.

73. Cam - a mechanical cam working in a timer.

74. Car - a very jazzy car.

75. Coal - large lumps of coal.

76. Cash - a stack of greenbacks
in their wrappings.

77. Cake - a ten-tiered wedding
cake.

78. Cuff - a cuff on a pants leg.

79. Cap - a graduation cap.

80. Face - a clown's face.

81. Fat - Two very fat sumo
wrestlers.

82. Fan - an electric fan.

83. Fame - a trophy on a
mantle.

84. Fare - a fare box on a bus.

85. Fall - a soccer player falling.

86. Fish - a goldfish in a bowl.

87. Fig - a bunch of figs.

88. Fife - a revolutionary
soldier playing a fife.

89. Fob - a watch fob dangling
from a waist.

90. Base - the first base bag.

91. Bat - Babe Ruth at bat.

92. Bean - a pile of string beans.

93. Beam - a beam of light from a
lighthouse.

94. Bar - a few bars of gold.

95. Ball - a soccer ball zooming into the net.

96. Badge - a large policeman's badge.

97. Back - a man getting his back massaged.

98. Beef - a beef steak sizzling on the grill.

99. Baby - a flying stork carrying a newborn.

100. Thesis - a stack of typewritten

pages with a blue ribbon around them.

Well, that list will give you something to chew on for a while. After you compose your word pictures and go through the list a few times, you will see that the job is not as difficult as you first pictured it.

The complete list of the primary and secondary key words is:

1. Tea	Hut	35. Mail	Mule	68. Chef	Chief
2. Noah	Hen	36. Match	Mesh	69. Chip	Chop
3. May	Ham	37. Mike	Mug	70. Case	Kiss
4. Ray	Hare	38. Muff	Movie	71. Cat	cot
5. Law	Hole	39. Map	Mop	72. Can	Cone
6. Jaw	Hedge	40. Race	Rose	73. Cam	Comb
7. Key	Hook	41. Rat	Rod	74. Car	Crow
8. Fee	Hoof	42. Rain	Ruin	75. Coal	Coil
9. Bay	Hoop	43. Ram	Room	76. Cash	Couch
10. Toes	Daisy	44. Rear	Rower	77. Cake	Coke
11. Tot	Deed	45. Rail	Reel	78. Cuff	Calf
12. Tan	Den	46. Rash	Roach	79. Cap	Cape
13. Tam	Dam	47. Rake	Rock	80. Face	Fuse
14. Tar	Deer	48. Reef	Roof	81. Fat	Foot
15. Tail	Dial	49. Rope	Rabbi	82. Fan	Phone
16. Tissue	Dish	50. Lace	Lasso	83. Fame	Foam

17. Tack	Duck	51. Lot	Lid	84. Fare	Fur
18. Taffy	Dove	52. Lane	Lion	85. Fall	File
19. Tap	Dip	53. Lime	Lamb	86. Fish	Fudge
20. Nose	Noose	54. Lair	Lure	87. Fig	Fog
21. Net	Nude	55. Lily	Lilli	88. Fife	Five
22. Noon	Nun	56. Lash	Leech	89. Fob	FAB
23. Name	Nome	57. Lake	Lock	90. Base	Pass
24. Nero	Winner	58. Leaf	Loaf	91. Bat	Pot
25. Nail	Nile	59. Lap	Lip	92. Bean	Pan
26. Niche	Notch	60. Chase	Cheese	93. Beam	Palm
27. Neck	Nook	61. Chat	Sheet	94. Bar	Pear
28. Navy	Knife	62. Chain	Shin	95. Ball	Pail
29. Nap	Nip	63. Chime	Jam	96. Badge	Peach
30. Mass	Moose	64. Chair	Shore	97. Back	Peg
31. Mat	Maid	65. Chile	Shell	98. Beef	Puff
32. Man	Moon	66. Judge	Choo-choo	99. Baby	Pope
33. Mama	Mummy	67. Check	Chick	100. Thesis	Disease
34. Mare	Mare				

The secondary list, starting with Hut, can be used for the numbers 101 to 200. So if you have a list of 200 items, you would know that a hut represents 101 and not 1. Or, if you had to learn two successive lists of 100 items, you would use the secondary key words as the alternate list for the numbers 1 to 100.

To have the least amount of confusion, the silent consonant h is used for 101 to 109. For 110 to 119, I used a d instead of a t. For 190 to 199, I used a p instead of a b.

On each key word list, only the number 34 uses the same picture word. I just couldn't find a better word for 34 on the secondary list.

Lily is a flower. Lilli is a well-bred lady of the 1890's with a huge hat.

FAB is a brand of soap.

For the numbers 49, 53, 78, and 89, I would have reversed the picture words, putting the one with the "a" vowel on the primary list, but I did not devise the primary list.

I use both the primary and the secondary Numerical Order Alphabets in my memory stage shows, and I can truthfully say that it took me only a couple months to feel confident that I could count to 200 by objects instead of by numbers.

SHOWER UP AN ALPHABET OR TWO

Each morning while taking a shower I do 100 belly pulls to exercise my abdominal muscles. I count the belly pulls using the Numerical Order Alphabet, alternating between the primary and secondary sets each time. Some people call this overlearning, but I call it refreshing my memory.

I suggest you find ways to refresh your memory by repeating the alphabet at least once each day. The belly-pull method may not be for you, but I promise, you will feel great when you can count by key words to 100 without looking at your list.

How about pasting the list on your bathroom mirror and on your refrigerator.

A TRIP TO THE GROCERY

Consider this situation: You have just learned the names of the sixteen rifles for the test that you'll take in two days. But you need to go shopping and don't want to use a written list of the 20 items you need to buy. You can't use the first sixteen key words, since you don't want to replace a rifle with a watermelon. You haven't yet committed the secondary list of key words to memory. What do you do?

Start with 21 (Net) and go to 40 (Race).

Here is the grocery list:

Watermelon

Lettuce

Tomatoes

Muffins

Bananas

Eggs

Garlic

Corn

Mustard

Onions

Celery

Napkins

Grapes

Tide

Bagels

Carrots

Milk

Chicken

Pineapple

Bread

Associate these items with your key words from 21 to 40. Take five minutes. I'll go fry an egg while you hook these items to your key words.

Time's up. We'll come back later to see how many you remember.

Turn to the next chapter.

I remember your name perfectly, but I just
can't think of your face.

Reverend W. A. Spooner

CHAPTER EIGHT

LINKING FOR LONGER NUMBERS

The easiest way to tell a guy how to remember
all the things he has done wrong - just have him
ask his wife.

You wish to remember the number 567. How do you do it <u>with the key words you know</u>? You could combine <u>jaw</u> with <u>check</u> and picture a jaw resting on a check book by separating the digits by 5 and 67. Or you could visualize a <u>lash</u> around a <u>key</u> by separating them by 56 and 7.

You want to remember the number 4293. How do you do it <u>with the key words you know</u>? You can separate the digits by twos: 42 93. Your key words would be <u>rain</u> and <u>beam</u>. You could picture it raining down from a beam.

In each of these examples, the problem is that weeks or months after you made the association you might not remember which key word came first.

To solve the problem of which set of digits comes first, use the primary Numerical Order Alphabet for the first two digits of a three- or four-digit number and the secondary Numerical Order Alphabet for the remaining digit or digits.

For example: 4293 would be visualized as <u>rain</u> falling on an open <u>palm</u>. The number has to be 4293 rather than 9342 because rain is in the primary Numerical Order Alphabet. Cool?
Another example: 114 would be remembered by breaking it down to 11 and 4 - <u>tots</u> and <u>hare</u>.

These methods of remembering three and four digits are basic ways of <u>linking</u>. You have linked one key word with another. Your story consists of two picture words.

The <u>Link Method</u> consists of the linking of two or more picture words into a sentence, poem or story.

With these examples, I emphasized using the key words you already know. By using key words you already know, you have instant hooks upon which to attach items or numbers you want to remember.

WHAT'S IN THE BACK?

What if you want to use one word to represent a three-digit number, such as 446? A person could spend all day trying to find a word which phonetically becomes 446. Right. So I've made it easy for you. I went to the English dictionary and found all the words or combinations of words whose first three consonants sound as a 446. I listed them in a special dictionary - the *Dictionary of Word/Number Conversions* [Appendix E]. The listed words are:

arrearage, irracial, reregister, a rare show, and reregiment.

All you would need to do is pick one from this special dictionary that works best for you.

In the *Dictionary of Word/Number Conversions* I have listed many of the words in the English dictionary which can be transposed into one-, two- and three-digit numbers. It's okay to take a quick peek at them. When you have time to look up picture words for three-digit numbers, this dictionary is an excellent reference source.

Because this special dictionary is included in this book, never let the book out of your hands. WARNING! The dictionary is too valuable to lose -- you'll be referring to it forever. Let your friends buy their own copies.

So, for three-digit numbers, you have the choice of using the picture words of the primary and secondary Numerical Order Alphabets or by picking words from the *Dictionary of Word/Number Conversions.*

WHAT'S THE LONG STORY?

What if you have a longer series of numbers to remember? What if you had to remember the 64th power of two [two multiplied by itself 64 times]?

The number is:

18446744073709551616

Don't throw up your arms in despair. You know I'll show you how easy it is.

My cue system is to coin a short story linking the picture words representing the digits. I composed, "The chair thief reregisters career and schemes to explain loyalty in a hugeditch."

Any time you ask me for the 64th power of two, I will immediately respond with all 20 digits of this very long number (18 quintillion) because I have combined linking with hooking.

The key word is chair. It is the 64th word in the primary Numerical Order Alphabet. To this picture word I hooked the remainder of my story, starting with thief - the word I chose to represent the first two of the 20 digits.

Obviously, there is no word in the English dictionary which can be transposed or converted to the remaining digits. So I broke the number into a series of three-digit numbers preceded by one two-digit number, as follows:

18 446 744 073 709 551 616

Then I converted the number 18 to thief. It wasn't too difficult to find a word which sounds like 18. From the *Dictionary of Word/Number Conversions* I had my choice of:

taffy, dove, thief, thieve, tough, deaf, defy and daffy.

Thief worked well for the sentence I intended to construct.

[You might question why I didn't stick with taffy or dove from the Numerical Order Alphabets instead of now abandoning all that I laid out for you in the previous chapters. The answers are: 1) that the Numerical Order Alphabets are used for short-term memory recall while linking can be used for longer-term memory recall, and 2) by giving you more choices for linking words, you can better construct meaningful sentences or stories and also avoid using the same key words too often].

Next, I converted each group of three digits into a word.

I have already shown you how I listed in the *Dictionary of Word/Number Conversions* many of the words that phonetically represent 446. Again, they are:

arrearage, irracial, reregister, a rare show, and reregiment.

I chose reregister, as it seemed to fit in with the available words for the other sets of three-digit numbers to make a story which I could memorize.

The resulting linked story was:

"The chair thief reregisters career and schemes to explain loyalty in a hugeditch."

Since I frequently refresh my memory for the powers of two to the 64th power, I don't believe I will ever forget this sentence or the 64th power of two.

Want to impress your friends with your improved memory? Let them ask you for any power of two up to the 64th power, and you reel off all the digits.

TO SUM IT UP

Here are the sums for the powers of two up to the 64th power:

1)---2	33)---8 589 934 592
2)---4	34)---17 179 869 184
3)---8	35)---34 359 738 368
4)---16	36)---68 719 476 736
5)---32	37)---137 438 953 472
6)---64	38)---274 877 906 944
7)---128	39)---549 755 813 888
8)---256	40)---1 099 511 627 776
9)---512	41)---2 199 023 255 552
10)---1 024	42)---4 398 046 511 104
11)---2 048	43)---8 796 093 022 208
12)---4 096	44)---17 592 186 044 416

13)---8 192	45)---35 184 372 088 832
14)---16 384	46)---70 368 744 177 664
15)---32 768	47)---140 737 488 355 328
16)---65 536	48)---281 474 976 710 656
17)---131 072	49)---562 949 953 421 312
18)---262 144	50)---1 125 899 906 842 624
19)---524 288	51)---2 251 799 813 685 248
20)---1 048 576	52)---4 503 599 627 370 496
21)---2 097 152	53)---9 007 199 254 740 992
22)---4 194 304	54)---18 014 398 509 481 984
23)---8 388 608	55)---36 028 797 018 963 968
24)---16 777 216	56)---72 057 594 037 927 936
25)---33 554 432	57)---144 115 188 075 855 872
26)---67 108 864	58)---288 230 376 151 711 744
27)---134 217 728	59)---576 460 752 303 423 488
28)---268 435 456	60)---1 152 921 504 606 846 976
29)---536 870 912	61)---2 305 843 009 213 693 952
30)---1 073 741 824	62)---4 611 686 018 427 387 904
31)---2 147 483 648	63)---9 223 372 036 854 775 808
32)---4 294 967 296	64)---18 446 744 073 709 551 616

Don't go into shock. You don't have to start converting these numbers. I've already done it for you.

Here are the hooks and links I use to impress my audiences with my "powerful" memory:

1 - 4. No hooks and links necessary. I could multiply this much in my head.

5. Law man.

6. Jaw jeer.

7. Key tinfoil.

8. Fee knowledge.

9. Bay lightning.

10. Toes tow snare.

11. Tots own a serf.

12. Tan her specie.

13. Tams have debentures.

14. Tar is on the Dutch mover.

15. Tale of money - a cageful.

16. Tissue and shawl are illmatched.

17. Tack the tomato skin.

18. Taffy is in the ancient drawer.

19. Tap the liner unfavorably.

20. Nose to survey the luggage.

21. Net no spook outline.

22. It's the noon hour - daybreak was miserable.

23. Name. View the moviefied Joseph.

24. Nero, touch the kicking nightwatchman.

25. With a nail, maim the well-larded airman.

26. In the niche is a jug with an adhesive fisher.

27. On the neck is a tumor on the intoxicated convict.

28. In the navy an unshaved armhole is relished.

29. They're napping - the illmatched foxes and python.

30. The masses heed the scheme to crowd the funeral.

31. On the mat, the <u>hen</u> and the turkey are refamiliarized by the sheriff.

32. Man, <u>hurry</u> the unburdened pushcart with no inhibition.

33. Mama, wave at the lifeboat in the bomber in the oilpainting.

34. The mare is eating decapitated at the fishpond in Dover.

35. Mail Mary a mulberry with a comfortable mi-shave.

36. Match. Shave an octopus aircushion by a commissioner.

37. Mic demagogs remove the blame in Oregon.

38. The muff engraved with a Viking is in possession of the bearer.

39. Map the larboard Galilee fathom and vivify.

40. Race the hot soapbubble to the lighted junction cocksure.

41. Rats <u>win</u> and depopulate the cinema. Unloyal Lillian.

42. Rain is <u>here</u>. The impoverished sergeant eluded the desert.

43. The rams <u>heave</u> the cabbage a submerged seaonion
    unsafely.

44. Rear. <u>Take</u> the alpine whitefish swearer a radish.

45. Rail mill deformity magnifies. Seefive halfmoons.

46. Get the rash gauze. A matchful career is in attacking joshers.

47. With a rake, terrace combing revives maylillies manifold.

48. On a reef an invading recruit's bookish kites shilly-shally.

49. The rope on a legendary parapet is blemished by an oriental mutiny.

50. Lace. <u>Hide</u> in the tunnel at halfbob position, a French general.

51. In a lot, a <u>hen</u> unloads copybooks while footmen shuffle nervously.

52. In a lane, <u>her</u> wholesome leap-up at the junction makes a rupture.

53. Eat a lime and <u>be</u> seasick. Topboots kneeler cruises to   Pepin.

54. In a lair, a dove stares at an impoverished Lisbon raft beaver.

55. The lily's image was sniffed. Copying the staff is a bushman with a pitchfork.

56. Lash the canoe slack. The leopard smokes the pink bombshell.

57. In the lake, in a hydroairplane, a total of eighty-five scholars flail
     an afghan.

58. A leaf anfive is an unmistakable makeshift toilet. Cathedral is careworn.

59. Lap, languish and rejoice in clinics and museums. Uranium revives.

60. Chasers <u>hate</u> Italian bands. Losers in cheeseshop is a fresh picture.

61. Chat. <u>Noah</u> mislaid the fireman's suspenders in a nightmare on shipmate's
     plantation.

62. Chain <u>hero</u>. Judith's chevy-chaser's stiff warning is moving passersby.

63. Chimed <u>by</u> the anonymous Mohegan who smashed the flier's goggles
     phosphor.

64. The chair thief re-register's career and schemes to explain loyalty in
     a hugeditch.

[I underlined a few small words so that I wouldn't skip over them when
reciting the numbers].

It is important for you to understand why and when we use three-digit
picture words instead of combinations from the Numerical Order Alphabets. I
want to re-emphasize that we avoid overuse and displacement by using three-
digit picture words for <u>linking</u>, for the *Dictionary of Word/Number Conversions*
gives us access to a very large number of words so that no linking poem or story
should be similar to any other. Because of the dissimilarities of such poems or
stories, linking allows us longer-term memory recall.

The Numerical Order Alphabets are best used for <u>hooking</u>, since they are
best used for short-term memory recall and for when we need to know the
numerical order of the items on the list.

Interestingly, memorizing the Powers of Two allows us to use both
<u>hooking</u> and <u>linking</u>. Our hooks were the picture words from 1 to 64. To those
hooks, we attached the linking sentences for each of the sums. Because the
hooked items are sentences unlike any others, rather than single objects,
displacement does not occur and the entire combination will remain in long-term
memory.

CHALLENGES

What do you do if 1) your friends decide to challenge your memory by giving you a long number to remember or if 2) you are the rare person who will need to remember a long number thrown out to you by a member of an audience?

With either case, you will have a problem. You will not have available the *Dictionary of Word/Number Conversions* to find words which translate into each group of three digits. But in these cases, since you need to remember the link only momentarily, you should work with groups of two-digit numbers.

Suppose you were asked to remember the number

46903917364758697.

Naturally, you would ask the person to repeat the digits very slowly. You would break the number down into 46 90 39 17 36 47 58 69 and 7. Your key words from the primary Numerical Order Alphabet are:

rash, base, map, tack, match, rake, leaf, chip and key.

As each group of two digits were spoken, you would need to link the key words together.

You could visualize a <u>rash</u>-covered arm sliding into a first <u>base</u> shaped like a <u>map</u>. The first-baseman puts a <u>tack</u> into your arm and lights it with a <u>match</u>. He <u>rakes</u> <u>leaves</u> over your arm. He takes a bat and <u>chips</u> a <u>key</u> over it. Voila! You have recalled a number with 17 digits and needed only 9 key words to link it together.

A stage performer who does this act every night might make these associations quick enough and remember them long enough to wow an audience. It takes practice, practice and practice. You'd better have a lot of practice before you let your friends challenge you.

For the average person who wants to improve his memory, and who doesn't have to perform, the three-digit method is much easier and the linking will remain in memory for a much longer time.

The nice thing about redundancy, the overlapping of the several systems, is that you have choices. There is no hard and fast rule that you must use the two-digit system or the three-digit system in certain situations. Use the system or the alphabet which works best for you in each situation.

NOT TIRED?

Want to remember phone numbers - it's no problem, even though they now consist of 10 digits. Since you are about to finish this chapter, you can skip to Chapter Eighteen if you want to work some more with longer numbers.   But first...

TEST TIME

You ask what am I testing now? Did you forget already? "Begin the Beguine" by slowly saying aloud the key words for the numbers 21 to 40. Don't they bring back memories? Like having some vegetables or fruit attached to them? Ah, yes, the grocery list. How well have you remembered the grocery list from the last chapter? Get a pen and paper and go to it.

CHAPTER NINE

ORGANIZATION OF MATERIALS

How do you know if you really have a bad memory?

A patient came to me with that problem. His wife had just returned from a visit to her doctor. She couldn't remember if he diagnosed Alzheimer's or Aids. My patient wanted to know what he should do. I suggested that he drive his wife out into the desert and drop her off. I said that if she finds her way home, he shouldn't sleep with her.

Organizing materials is a significant aid to memory. The term organization includes the processes of summarizing, outlining and classifying. Unfortunately, most people do not utilize this methodology. But you, from now on, will make a conscious effort to organize information.

Let's see how to engage in the process.

I know you've read the first eight chapters of this memory book, learned and memorized the materials, and you have become an expert with the Hook Method and the Link Method. Forget it all.

I don't really mean for you to forget it. I mean just pretend for the moment. If you learned and practiced what I've taught, your new knowledge will fade from your mind only if you fail to refresh your memory periodically or you fail to apply the new knowledge.

Try not to think about all you have read and learned. Assume the following is the first of my tests.

A NEW LIST

Read the following list of objects for just a few seconds. Do not make any associations. No hooks. No links. Then close the book and write on a sheet of paper all those you can remember.

principal	jeans	poem	soccer
football	classroom	playground	shirt
socks	tennis	tie	teacher
novel	screenplay	baseball	short story

Close the book and write the items you remember.

Geez, you've already re-opened the book, and I didn't even have the time to grab a cup of coffee. You owe me.

Well, how many did you remember? If you recalled more than eight, you are exceptional. If you didn't remember more than four, I'm going to put you in line for a brain transplant.

In about the same amount of time as it took for you to read the list, you could have observed that the sixteen items can be grouped into four categories: school, sports, clothing and writing. By classifying the items into these meaningful categories, you would have improved your recall by using the categories as cue words to trigger your memory.

I would have classified the items as:

School	Sports	Clothing	Writing
principal	football	socks	novel
classroom	tennis	jeans	screenplay
playground	baseball	tie	poem
teacher	soccer	shirt	short story

CRYBABY?

Of course, I only gave you a few seconds and didn't clue you in on classifying - that's why you didn't do well. But isn't this chapter titled "Organization of Materials" and didn't the first paragraph speak about classifying materials?

Don't feel too bad. I was told once that my brain was so small that if I had two of them, I still couldn't blow my nose. Perhaps that's why I write with a nasal twang.

ANOTHER CHANCE

Let's try another group to get you in rhythm.

I'm assuming you are computer literate - I'll give you the benefit of any doubt.

Take a few extra seconds after you read through the following list and see if you can find four categories to separate the items into. Before you close the book, write on a sheet of paper the categories you think are best. Then review the list one more time.

program	keyboard	bulletin board	disk
modem	file	scanner	desktop
printout	e-mail	CD	monitor
chat room	tape	folder	search

Do it, and close the book.

Write the items you recall.

Bet you did better this time in recalling them. Into what categories did you classify them? I'll give you my answer shortly.

That's the organizing system. It requires your decision to start classifying information as soon as you hear it or read it. Don't wait until after a lecture or article is completed and your notes finished. Think in terms of classification of ideas as the lecture proceeds. To be able to classify information, that information first must be boiled down to its essence. Most books or speeches probably could be condensed to just a few pages of the important points. As a reader or as a listener, it is our job to do the condensing. This requires that we summarize the material.

Once we have performed the summarization, we need to outline the major points, much as an author prepares a table of contents for a book.

When the outline is completed, then we can classify information from within the outline.

With the list I provided you above, assume that the items were derived after summarization and outlining of a book on elementary education.

ONE WAY OF DOING IT

I suggest classifying the list this way:

Hardware	Internet Services	Software	Backup
modem	chat room	program	printout
keyboard	e-mail	file	tape
scanner	bulletin	board folder	disk
monitor	search	desktop	CD

Separating items into four categories may be practical for short lists of perhaps ten to forty items, but when you get larger numbers of items, they should be sub-classified.

For example: If you want to put up a website on Internet to be a directory of screenplays offered for sale by writers, you might classify them by genre, such as by thriller, horror, detective, comedy, drama and adolescent.

As your list of writers grows, you might sub-classify the list as to 1) low budget, 2) medium budget and 3) we'll go bankrupt if we spend this much.

Another way of classifying which might be of interest to producers seeking good scripts would be to further sub-divide by whether the lead character is male or female, or by whether it is an ensemble project with no lead actors versus having a star in a lead role.

Some producers are more interested in who has written the screenplay. They might want to conduct their search by screenwriters, so you could have a separate classification for that.

Got the idea?

You can check out www.memorysite.com/screenplays on the Internet to see how Allworld Screenplays is currently classifying writers and services associated with writers.

PRACTICE, PRACTICE, PRACTICE

At your leisure, think about those areas of knowledge which interest you - whether it be sports, entertainment, business or whatever-floats-your-boat. Break down and organize your knowledge into categories.

Want to know if this really will improve your memory and help you get ahead? Let me tell you a true story.

STORY TIME

When I was in law school, I worked my way through. Between work, classes and sleep I had no time to read any law cases. Since I had no time to read and re-read extensive notes, I didn't take them. I spent only a total of eight hours in the law library during the entire three years. Professors knew not to call on me to detail a case, because I never could.

Fortunately for me, grades were based solely on how well one did on the final examination.

So what I did do was to write a short sentence at the end of each class summarizing the essence of the law dealt with during that hour. If the hour were spent discussing a precedent-setting case, I would draw a picture representing that day's principle of law and a picture substitute for the name of the case.

DO DEER HAVE ADAM'S APPLES?

For example: If the case were Adams vs. Doe, I would draw a picture of a deer with a large Adam's apple. If the rule of law from that case stated you couldn't enter a premise without knocking, I would draw a door knocker. I then connected the two with an arrow.

My intent was that if I were to be queried about Adams vs. Doe, I would visualize the deer with the Adam's apple and the door knocker. It would be enough clues for me to remember the rule of law of the case.

At the end of the course I had a very thin notebook, which I then outlined, based on my one sentence summaries and my drawings. From 4:00 A.M. to 7:45 A.M. on the morning of the final exam, I would read my summaries and outline and refresh my picture associations.

Meanwhile, nearly all my classmates had volumes of notebooks in which they had detailed the facts of all the cases. They had to spend days and even weeks trying to condense and re-condense their notes.

At 7:45 A.M. I trotted over to the classroom, the material fresh in my short-term memory, and I did fairly well on each exam. So much for background information.

Constitutional Law is one the of the longest and most important courses in law school. It ran for a full three quarters (two semesters). If you received a good grade in Con Law, it would offset a number of poor grades in other courses. Professor Strong told my class on the first day of the course that anyone who determined how the Supreme Court decided cases would get an A in the course.

The night before the final and only exam, I typed one and one-half pages of narrative and drew a triangular diagram. Attached to each of the three points of the triangle, I linked a picture word to illustrate a methodology I believed applied to the Supreme Court. Outside each corner I gave a brief rationale. Inside the triangle, I wrote, "Supreme Court Decisions and Rationales." I labelled the diagram, "The Map of the Supreme Court." The next morning I submitted my effort to Professor Strong.

I haven't seen the drawing since, and I don't remember now what my points were because my mother threw out my little essay along with a lot of other good stuff - even my prized Boy Scout merit badge sash - when she did spring housecleaning.

No one else in the Con Law class submitted an explanation - they were too busy trying to re-read their volumes of notes.

I also used the triangular diagram as part of my memory tool for taking the examination.

After Professor Strong graded all the exam papers, he called me into his office. I thought I had flunked the course because the exam was very difficult.

The professor said he knew he had promised an A to anyone who could determine how the Supreme Court decided cases. But I had scored only a C on the exam. He asked if I would accept a B for the course instead of the A.

I readily accepted, and got the hell out of there before he changed his mind.

That's how I became a lawyer. Professor Strong became dean of the Ohio State University law school.

If you ask me now what else of interest occurred during my year in the Con Law class, I would draw a blank. I remembered this occurrence because it was an important event in my life, and I have thought about it many times since. This refreshing of my memory moved it from short-term memory into long-term memory and prevented fading.

MAPPING FOR MEMORY

In those early days, I called the pictures I drew "mapping for my memory." I'm sure that description was not original with me - but I don't know where I came in contact with the concept of mapping. This technique has been improved, polished and codified by people such as Tony Buzan, author of many books on memory, who thirty years later coined the word "Mind-Mapping" for it.

A very nice description of "Mapping for Memory" by Wayne Lundberg, an expert on mapping, is set out in Chapter Eleven.

WHERE IS YOUR NOTEBOOK?

This takes us to the subject of notebooks and diaries.

What if some events of lesser importance had occurred during that freshman year in law school, which ordinarily would only and did only get into intermediate-term memory? If I had been smart enough then, I would have maintained a LIFE EXPERIENCE'S NOTEBOOK. I would have listed in it occurrences to remember and the names of people who had notable importance to my life. Where possible, I would have drawn pictures representing those events or people.

Periodically over the years I would have refreshed my memories. Even if I became lazy, the notebooks would have been available at any time for reference.

I distinguish a Life Experience's Notebook from a diary in that the latter usually consists of extensive notes for each day and details thinking processes and emotions. The Notebook should consist of brief notes and drawings, which might be entered perhaps only once a month, if nothing of importance were occurring. One notebook might cover a period of several years - it would be easy to preserve.

Well, I wasn't smart enough back then to start a Life Experiences Notebook. But it's no excuse for you, if you don't start one today.

Interestingly though, I have preserved my telephone and address books going back to 1953. They were small, and I just threw the old one into a shoe box when I started a new one - usually when I moved or changed office locations. Today I have Rolodex's. When I look back over the names of people I listed in those old books, memories start to flow into my conscious mind; memories I have not had access to for decades. All just by association with names now in my consciousness from those books.

So, besides starting your Life Experiences' Notebook today, you might get an old shoe box and start preserving your personal phone books or Rolodex's of names and numbers.

TEST TIME

Here's a list of cars and trucks for a classification exercise. Take your time. Break down the vehicles into categories.   Since most people would not be familiar with the entire list, I'm giving you permission to look at the newspaper pages which advertise cars for sale.

When you are finished, check your answers with mine in Appendix A.

Nissan King Cab

Dodge Caravan

GMC Suburban

Cadillac Seville

Ford Escort

Chevy Malibu

Plymouth Voyager

Toyota 4Runner

Infinity sedan

Mercedes sedan

Chevy Silverado

Ford Explorer

Toyota Camry

Chevy Astro

Ford Ranger

Land Rover

Ford Winstar

Toyota Tacoma

Hyundai Accent

"When they begin the Beguine
It brings back the sound of music so tender,
It brings back a night of tropical splendour,
It brings back a memory ever green."

Cole Porter, 1935

CHAPTER TEN

ORGANIZING AND LINKING FOR DELIVERING SPEECHES

This week I wanted to practice on my memory, so
I memorized five pages of the Los Angeles phone book.
Want to hear the names I committed to memory? Garcia, Garcia, Garcia,
Garcia and Hernandez.

In Chapter Eight we used the Link Method to recall a long series of digits. The Link Method follows a more or less straight line from one item to the next, just as a screenplay moves from one scene to the next.

In Chapter Nine we saw that organization by summarizing, outlining and classifying items is a completely different way to aid recall. We spent much of the time dealing with classifying items; little attention was given to outlining.

In this chapter we will discuss summarization and outlining and show how the Linking Method is not only for use with long numbers, but also is an essential element of outlining.

For books which are lengthy, it would be a Herculean task to summarize and outline every thought or action. So when we engage in the summarization stage, we should sift out the lesser points before writing the summary and outline.

Generally, the author will have separated the major thoughts or actions into individual chapters, often with chapter captions. Those captions usually form the table of contents of the book. One need only turn to the table of contents to obtain a good summary and outline of the book. The step of linking the outline then becomes a slam dunk.

For example: The following is the table of contents for ERICA WILSON'S KNITTING BOOK, Erica Wilson, Charles Scribner's Sons, 1988.

CONTENTS

TEXTURE

<u>Soft Cable</u>

>How to Make a Soft Cable

>Soft Cable Sweater

<u>Skye</u> Stitches

>How to Make Skye Stitches

>Skye Sampler Sweater

>Skye Blue Sweater

<u>Lattice Pattern</u>

>How to Make the Lattice Pattern

>Sea Mist Sweater

<u>Lacy</u> Cable

>How to Make the Lacy Cable Pattern

>Lacy Cable Pullover

<u>Eyelet</u> Lace

>How to Make Eyelet Lace

>Pinafore

>Child's Victorian Yoke Dress

>Child's Classic Dress

Lace <u>Leaves</u>

>How to Make the Lace Leaves Pattern

>Pink Cloud Sweater

<u>Cascading Waterfall</u>

>How to Make the Cascading Waterfall Pattern

>Cascading Waterfall Sweater

How to Embroider Your Finished Sweater

Nantucket Sweater

Bands, Borders, and Bullions

Tyrolean Embroidered Jacket

Duplicate Stitch

How to Do Duplicate Stitch

Evening Rose Sweater

Autumn Leaves Sweater

Child's "Find the Letter" Sweater

Textured Effects

Textured Effects--Smocking, Spool-Kitting, and Applique.

Smocked Dress

Child's Snakes and Ladders Cardigan

Child's Humpty-Dumpty Sweater

Blocking and Caring for Your Sweater

Taking Your Measurements

Things You Need to Know

Measurements and Suppliers

Knitter's Graph Paper

If I had to deliver a review of this book to a ladies' sewing club, I probably would be the only man in the room. I would want to do the job without notes. "I'll show them knitting is not just for women."

I would read the Contents over several times to get a feel for what the author is doing.

From Erica Wilson's Contents, it appears that for each main topic, she has described how to perform the operation. Then she gives one or more examples of what can be made using each method. Ah-ha. I could show slides of each example, and then I wouldn't need to memorize them. It would cut my job in half! Besides, a picture is worth a thousand words.

Next, I would underline the words in the Contents which I consider important as <u>cue words</u>. These are words which highlight or represent the major ideas. If you will look at the Contents, you will note that I've already underlined those cue words. (Writing on a word processor makes it very easy to go back and do things like this, as if I thought of it when I first typed the Contents).

Using the underlined cue words, I have linked them together into a series of <u>Linking Paragraphs</u>, as follows:

The history of knitting covers the tools, basic knitting and easy projects like sweaters, hats and scarfs that are not crocheted.

The soft cable in the sky stitches a lattice pattern on a sweater made of leaves and lazy eyelets, like a cascading waterfall.

The honeycombed hexagon diamond weaved bubbles and bands and weaved patterns which had to change bobbins for jazzy knitting.

Embroider the bands and borders. A bullion in duplicate for textured effects.

If you block your sweater, take your measurements and know it all, suppliers will print your name on knitting graph paper for all the world to see.

Five easy paragraphs to memorize. Taken together, they become a story or a poem. Having gone over them several times a day for a week before the speech, I would have the story down pat.

Also, to key the paragraphs I would visualize one picture which would include 1) a sweater with knitting needles and a spool of yarn embroidered on its front, 2) a cable attached to the sweater and reaching up toward a sweater made of leaves in the sky, 3) attached to the sweater, a hexagon diamond with bubbles flowing out into a cloud, 4) a textured and honeycombed gold bar on top of the cloud, and 5) a yard stick sticking out at the top with a flag of graphic paper attached to it.

While memorizing the contents of the five paragraphs and the drawing representing the ideas expressed, I would be reading the book to get an understanding of the essence of each topic.

I'M READY FOR YOU, LADIES

At the Ladies Sewing Club, after flashing a few photos of finished products, I would ask the ladies if they would like to learn how to make the items. Then wow them with my knowledge of knitting. I'd mentally visualize the picture I structured and go from thought to thought. All without my ever having knitted a stitch. At the end, I'd have someone take my picture with groups of the ladies.

It's a win/win situation.

DO IT YOUR WAY

Of course, if your book or article is not accompanied by a table of contents, you'll have to write summaries of the essential ideas and prepare the outline. Perhaps you'll make a better outline than the author would have done, for the high points will be personal to you.

There is a distinct advantage in writing your own cue words. As discussed in Chapter One, the more senses involved in absorbing material, the better the material will be remembered. In addition to sight, you will involve the kinesthetic sense related to writing. And don't forget to speak aloud what you write. Even the search for cue words to represent the gist of each idea to form a linkage will better implant the idea in your memory through repetition.

When you repeat the linking paragraphs to memorize them, you should think of the idea each cue word represents. In this way, you not only memorize the linking, but you get a good grasp of the material the links represent.

I know what you would like to say to me now - you don't knit and you don't read books. How is this really going to help you?

A speech basically is no more than a spoken story or sermon. To deliver one without notes, you need only to 1) summarize the important points, 2) outline them, 3) choose cue words which represent the major points and 4) design the linking paragraphs. It's a piece of cake.

THE CHOICE BETWEEN HOOKS AND LINKS

On a number of occasions I have been asked why I don't use the Hook Method instead of the Link Method when outlining the important parts of a speech or a book.

So let's review the differences between hooking and linking.

1. When items such as objects, thoughts or concepts have a logical relationship to each other, the Link Method is preferred. Books and speeches usually contain a thread which connects all the information presented.

2. Whenever items are unconnected and have no apparent relationship, the Hook Method is preferred.

3. Items remembered with the Hook Method will be remembered only for short periods of time due to fading and displacement. It is the norm to want to remember the content of books and speeches for a long time.

4. Items remembered with the Link Method can be remembered for a longer period of time because

   1) displacement is minimal, since a new story or poem is used for each series of items to be remembered.

   2) because there is a logical relationship between those items.

5. All other requirements being equal, if it is necessary to remember any item out of sequence, the Hook Method is preferred because you can easily recall the numerical order of each item on the list.

For example: You need to know which item is 66th on the list. If you had used the Link Method, you would have to count each item from the beginning to determine which one the 66th was. With the Hook Method you just visualize a judge (66) and see what is attached to him.

PRACTICE, PRACTICE, PRACTICE

Here are three tables of contents. Practice your linking.

Table Number One

LOFT LIVING - RECYCLING WAREHOUSE SPACE FOR RESIDENTIAL USE, Kingsley C. Fairbridge and Harvey-Jane Kowal, Saturday Review Press/E.P. Dutton & Co., Inc., 1976.

CONTENTS

OUCH!

        What struck my mind when I first read this list of chapters was that just from the list, without reading any more of the book, I probably could deliver a talk for at least ten minutes and not appear to be a dummy. After that, my lack of specific knowledge would be exposed.

A tremendous amount of information has been given to us by the authors with their outline in the form of a table of contents.

Go ahead and see how well you can link the highpoints.

ANOTHER EASY ONE

The next table of contents also is very simple, but it provides much less information with which to work.

Table Number Two

WOODTURNING FOR CABINETMAKERS, Michael Dunbar, Sterling Publishing Co., Inc., New York, 1990.

CONTENTS

1. Exploring the Lathe

2. Lathe Tools

3. Sharpening Techniques

4. Safety

5. Turning Blanks

6. Basic Technique

7. Making the Elements

8. Turning Design and Procedure

9. Duplicating

10. Turning Green Wood

11. Off-Center Turnings

12. Reeds and Flutes

13. Spiral Turnings

14. Chair Stiles

15. Turning Discs

16. Knobs, Pulls, Pegs and Other Parts

> Do your linking.

THE KILLER

You knocked off the first two books pretty easily. I don't think you spent more than 15 minutes for each to choose your linking words and to make your poem or story. The next one is a killer.

Table Number Three

THE COMPLETE BOOK OF HOME WELDING, John Todd, Tab Books, Inc., Blue Ridge Summit, PA, 1986.

CONTENTS

1. Who is Doing Welding Now? Who Could Be?

> Welding for (Almost) Everybody

2. Projects You Can Do At Home

> A Home Welding Project Sampler

3. Getting Started

> Your Aptitudes--A Safe Place to Work--A Practical Place to Work--Expenses--Time

4. Equipment You Will Need

> Cutting--Layout and Fitup--Welding--Power Source Types--Wire Feed Welding--Shielding Gas--Cleaning

12. A Plan of Action

Get the idea--Formulate a Step-by-Step Plan--Make a Materials List--Gather the Materials--Make Your Layout--Cut and Form Parts--Fit and Assemble--Weld It--Finish as Required

13. Not Very Creative?

Recording Ideas--Making Plans

14. Tools

Hand Tools--Power Tools--Measuring Tools--Tools for Marking--Where to Get Tools

15. Some Useful Layout Techniques

A Working Surface--Lines and Points--Square Layouts--Dividing Lines, Arcs and Angles--Copying and Angle--Round Layouts--Irregular Curves--Triangulation--Patterns and Templates--Capacities

16. How to Cut and Form Metal

Cutting Steel--Cutting Metal in the Home Shop--Oxyacetylene Cutting, the Old Reliable--Other Fuel Gases--Sawing--Hole Saws--Snips and Pipe Cutters--Drills--thread Cutting Tools--Chisels and Punches--Abrasive (Frictional) Cutting--Files--Air Carbon Arc Cutting (AAC)--Special Cutting Electrodes--Forming Metal

17. Fitup and Distortion Control

Effects of Heat--Restraints--Welding and Distortion Stress--Controlling Distortion--Fitting Together T and Butt Joints--Jigs or Fixtures--Tack Welds--Four Basic Fabrications--Fitting Round and Cylindrical Shapes--Using Hammers and Wrenches--Making vs Having Fits

18. Are We Having Fun Yet

Too Much Too Soon--Too Complex--Too Many Parts--To Big or Heavy--Too Expensive--Too Demanding--Unfamiliar Material--The Failed Weld Syndrome--Poor Weld Appearance--Too Much Noise--Too Much Time Preparing

19. Finishing a Steel Project

Cleaning and Finishing--Finish Grinding--Filing--Paint and Other Surface Applications--Storing Uncoated Steel

20. When to Use Outside Services

> When Safety is Involved--When Special Equipment is Needed--Outside Welding Services

21. Fix It? Maybe

> Metal Identification--Some Basic Repair Techniques--What Not to Do--weld Repairs to Cast Iron--Welded Inserts--Plugging a Hole--Hard Facing--Threaded Pipe Connections--Thawing Pipes

22. Joining Wood to Metal

> Wood and Metal Combinations--Moisture--Fasteners and Other Hardware--Wood and Welding

Obviously, there is far too much material here to include in a speech. However, if one needs to speak on home welding, these contents could be summarized, outlined, cued and linked.

Some key areas to touch upon would be tools and equipment, types of welding such as SMAW, GMAW and FCAW, techniques of welding, uses of tools, and working with gasses.

Go ahead and see what you can do.

Send your linked paragraphs, stories or poems for any of these three tables of contents to me. If they are good, I'll try to include them in the next edition of this book.

DID YOU MAKE AN EFFORT?

If you didn't go through the process of analyzing how I linked the main topics of the knitting book, or if you didn't bother testing yourself with outlining, cueing and linking loft living, woodturning or welding, you will not get the full benefits of this book.

Although five paragraphs of a linking poem or story can be memorized, it may take too long to memorize all the linking paragraphs of a long speech.

So let's make it easier.

IT KEEPS GETTING EASIER

I love making things easier for you.

So, after you have organized your material by summarizing, outlining, cueing and linking, make it all come together by tying the linking paragraphs to each other with the Hooking Method.

I know I have just again emphasized that we don't use the Hook Method in outlining a book or a speech because it is best used for short-term memory recall. But we can use it in addition to linking.

Here's how.

I have used a very simple alphabet cue system many times when delivering long lectures on - you guessed it - on how not to forget. It's the BODY PARTS ALPHABET. I hook the cue words of the linked story to parts of my body and my clothing. As I touch my body parts or clothing, starting with my bald head, I recall the hooked cue word, and away I go. It works beautifully, and no one seems to notice I am touching these areas on purpose.

Here are the body parts I use (in order):

Scalp

Sideburns

Ears

Eyebrows

Nose

Upper lip

Lower lip

Chin

Neck

Left shoulder

Upper jacket pocket

Right jacket pocket

Belt

Right pants pocket

Going back to knitting, I might hook the linked story as follows:

Scalp — I picture a hammer hitting my head. It represents the tools.

Sideburns — I picture a hat on the side of my head with a scarf tied around it.

Ears — I see a cable coming out of my ear and going up to the sky where a sweater-like cloud is in a lattice pattern.

Eyebrows — Leaves are falling off my eyebrows like a waterfall.

Nose — Bees are going up my nose. Diamonds and bubbles are falling out.

Upper lip — I see a bobbin on my lip.

Lower lip — My lower lip looks like embroidery and it is crossed by bands. It is bordered by red lipstick.

Chin — My chin is textured gold.

Neck — I see a turtle-necked sweater around my neck with a block embroidered on it.

Left shoulder — A ruler sits on it.

Upper jacket pocket — A roll of graph paper sticks out of the pocket. My name is on top.

Right jacket pocket — A globe rests inside.

Belt — Not needed.

Right pants pocket — Not needed.

Another advantage of the Body Parts Alphabet is that it keeps my hands moving so I don't look like some stiff. I don't use my knees, socks or my feet in this alphabet. I would look silly bending over to touch them while delivering my speech to the United Nations Assembly.

WHAT'S UP NEXT, DOC?

In the next chapter, we are going to learn an innovative way to better organize material and to make vivid pictorial associations. We'll see how we can incorporate the use of color, geometric shapes and out-of-the-ordinary organization of materials to improve our memories and to assist us in strategic breakthrough thinking.

I should sing you a song of September
And of life dying down to an ember.
I should reminisce
About that and of this
But it's all too damn hard to remember.

John Miller, Talco, TX 75487

CHAPTER ELEVEN

MAPPING FOR MEMORY

By Wayne Lundberg[1]

I'm a lucky man. When I go out to eat, my wife
reminds me what foods I like.

Logic, our traditional way of thinking and note-taking, forces the mind to think sequentially. We were taught to take notes in an orderly fashion. The instructor, the manual, the movie starts with an introduction and then moves into stuff we need to know in order to understand what follows. Then we get into the meat of things. Logically. One, two, three, four.

But the mind does not work that way. The mind is an infinitely sophisticated, fully relational database which handles millions of bits of information at once and can actually compare each of the million bits with another zillion bits instantly. Not even a Super Cray can come close to this, even with hundreds of hours of computing time. The mind can process a seemingly unlimited number of images at once.

Words are different. Words must be converted into images then back into words. When we feed our brain with images instead of words, we increase our thinking and remembering capabilities.

What do you see in your mind's eye when you hear "Mona Lisa"? Or "Eifel Tower" or "The Declaration of Independence". If you can `see' these images instantly, then you are a candidate for a very effective memory tool, and one of the easiest to use. It's called Mapping for Memory.

Not that Mapping for Memory is a new invention, but it is a relatively new way of displaying images and diagrams so that the information they represent is easily absorbed and retained.

Mapping for Memory works very well for note-taking of speeches, for outlining articles and books, viewing an educational program, preparing a plan of action, working through ideas alone or in a group, and for delivering a speech.

HOW GOOD IS IT?

Recall is excellent because with one or two reviews later on retention should be over 60%. With three reviews nearly 80% retention is possible, even years later. Traditional rote learning based on logical note-taking has a half life of only days. Try listing the Ten Commandments from memory. Or the amendments to the Constitution. If you have not pegged them to some visual image, some memory hook, you will not remember them unless you use them frequently.

Dr. Amazing, in Chapter Nine (Organization of Materials) recalls how he used images and diagrams during his first year of law school. The method was not original with him, but he found it effective to depict the rules of law he wanted to retain in memory.

In 1974, Tony Buzan codified and improved the method of using images and diagrams in his book, "Use Both Sides of Your Brain." He coined the word, "Mind-Mapping" for the method.

The Wizard of Oz.

Four words which if you were brought up in the traditional American culture would evoke the whole story of a Kansas farm hit by a tremendous tornado and a little girl transported to a fabulous land with a yellow brick road, timid lions, squeaking tin men, witches and an old guy behind the curtains pulling the wool over everybody's eyes. The entire movie would pass before your inner-eye if you gave it enough time. Four words triggering a sequence of images lasting over an hour and a half.

The essence of making maps for memory is listening, seeing or thinking of something in image form, giving it a name or a title, and placing the image and title in a circle or balloon in the center of a page of paper. A number of other images and titles representing major subdivisions are then placed on the page near the center and linked to the center by lines.

GET THE PICTURE

Here is the basic form of a map for memory.

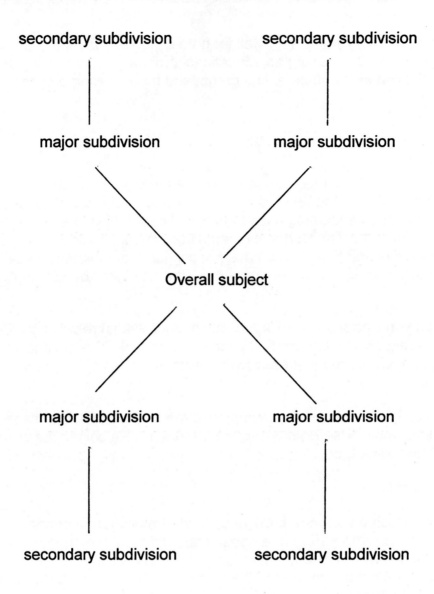

The old Chinese proverb is exactly right: A picture is worth a thousand words. When delivering a speech, a two to three word reminder along with the connecting balloons to other topics will enable your mind to spill those thousands of words in a logical, coherent, understandable manner. In the same way, when you later review memory-map notes, a simple sketch from your notes or a circled word will bring back the whole picture for instant recall.

RULES, RULES, RULES - ALWAYS RULES

Here are the fundamental rules of note-taking using mapping for memory principles as they exist today.

1- Rotate paper. Lay out the paper in a landscape fashion. Why? To tell your perception system that both right and left hemispheres are to play a role in what is to happen next.

2- Theme in the center and colored. Why? Everything to be written or sketched will now be put on paper according to the way you see the importance of the topic and not in a chronological order, as is typical with traditional note-taking.

For example: If we put the speaker's introductory notes on the very first lines on the top of the left-hand side of a standard note-book page, we are setting ourselves up for a false later review. We have been conditioned to see the first lines of anything as the most important. Give thanks to the newspaper type writing for this - Headline, lead, and a brief story of the whole in the first paragraph.

Using Mapping for Memory you are in control of where to put the most important and the least. I generally jot down the first topic after the theme to the right and mid-page as a start. The more important ideas should be closer to the center.

After a while, as I discover the key ingredients to the theme, they will be placed on the upper left corner of the page, where tradition dictates. That way, I have the advantage of both logic and the mapping of images.

3- The central theme should be enclosed in a geometric figure such as a triangle, square, rectangle, hexagon, pentagon. The number of major subdivisions of the theme should determine the shape of the figure. Each major subdivision can be attached to one of the points of the figure.

For example: A triangle would be used for a theme that has three major subdivisions.

You can also use geometric figures to enclose the ideas represented by each of the major subdivisions.

4- Use a four-color pen. Apply black, blue and green according to the way you will 'feel' about what you are making a note of. The more you are stimulated by color, shape and light, the more you will involve the internal sense of feeling. All images should have a color.

5- Use red only to make connections between ideas as you take notes. This red line or series of red lines connecting key thoughts and ideas will become the thread that brings lateral thinking into play. It is the Eureka![2]

6- A symbol is better than a word, a sketch better than a symbol. Try not to write more than four or five words per thought. The less words, the better. Words should be printed and not be in cursive, where the strokes of letters are joined in one word. By keeping words to a minimum we give the few words we use more power to kindle recall.

The basic structure of the map is open-ended, since it proceeds from a center point outward. This allows for the addition of new ideas without having to rewrite previous notes.

7- Doodle simple line drawings wherever possible next to the words or ideas. Not only on Mapping for Memory papers, but doodle and make lists whenever you have a chance.

Doodling is the activity primarily of the right hemisphere, the artistic side of us, the creative side.

As we begin to doodle, we also go through a transformation which an EEG would show as a shift from high-frequency brainwave activity to a lower frequency. Thus you are shifting to an altered state of consciousness, and powerful magic takes place in these regions. By working lists and sketches you invoke both hemispheres. The benefits are enormous.

8- Don't worry about how messy and unorganized it looks. Well organized notes are not conducive to improved memorization even though they may assist a student in getting a better grade while working in `traditional' environments. One reason Mapping for Memory is having a tough time catching on in the school system is that there is no way for a teacher to grade such papers.   How were Monet or Renoir graded when they showed their first paintings at the Salon des Refuses?[3]

9- Review your notes the following day or two and one week later. Again in six months for continued retention. Once we recall something two or three times using Mapping for Memory, we have locked in a synapse pathway and have memorized the material.

Notes and observations:

It is difficult for other people to understand your notes or be able to use them unless they participated in their creation. Yet, when you glance at a single page of notes having used Mapping for Memory, you will have near instant recall and can stand and deliver a fairly decent playback of what you heard, thought, read or brainstormed way back when you made the notes.

BREAKDOWN OF USES OF MAPPING FOR MEMORY

Uses:

1. Note taking in any classroom or seminar situation.

2. Capture brainstorming ideas in a manner which makes sense for later analysis.

3. Think of, organize and deliver a speech, a sermon, a presentation.

4. Invent something new. Strategic breakthrough thinking.

5. Problem solving alone or in a group

DON'T FORGET YOUR FOUR-COLORED PEN

Let's explore each use of Mapping for Memory in some detail.

1. Note taking in any classroom or seminar situation.

As a boy I discovered word and picture associations as a key tool in learning a new language and culture as well as for school. At seven I was taken to Mexico where from one day to the next I was immersed into a culture which made me feel as if I were a deaf, dumb and blind kid. I had to adapt fast or be left out. That move probably was the luckiest thing to occur in my life because I learned how to learn.

Later, in college, it amazed me how my fellow students would cram for exams while I would simply take the test, pass and go on to the next class and subject. I could not understand their panic and sleepless nights cramming for a test. Only later did I discover it was because they had not associated the daily class material with the previous - had not built knowledge brick by brick and image by image. They had been taught to memorize things by rote and it was the only way they had for passing tests. Cram, take the test, forget.

I may not remember the exact dates of many significant historical events, but I can visualize the settings, the clothes, the art, the science of the time and put it pretty much where it should be through visualization.

THANKS TO COLUMBUS

If it's really important to know that on October 12 in the year of our Lord 1492 Columbus discovered America, I know where to look it up. But for creative thinking, problem solving, or analysis, it is sufficient to know it was shortly after the Arabs were pushed back across the Straight of Gibraltar - which in turn triggers images of Constantinople, Venice and France. So I have a compass to guide me through the mire. How could a person who memorized dates without assigning images to the date have this ability?

The trick is to listen to the instructor and convert the lecture into images exactly as you would script a movie. As the instructor exposes this new knowledge, you should put it into perspective and add details as if you were a movie scriptwriter or director imagining the scenes. When a scene is firmly in place with action, color, setting, actors - then name it. Write the name on your note paper under the last picture which would logically connect the new image.

THE BIG EXAMPLE

For example: Your lecture today is Maslow's hierarchy of human needs. Fundamental stuff for anybody going into business or leadership fields. As the instructor ticks off the five levels of human needs, most students will write the following:

a) Food, clothing, shelter.

b) Security, regular paycheck, insurance, Army, Navy.

c) Society, sex, marriage, children, procreation.

d) Esteem, the need to feel worthy and respected.

e) Self actualization - when you know only God can see it.

In Mapping for Memory I would listen carefully, visualize a stage play with my ancestor beating a rabbit to death with a stick, lighting a fire, climbing a tree to protect himself from the jaguar, feeling all alone and wishing he had a playmate. I would see Jane in the next tree. They would talk, get together and make babies. They would find other families and join in a tribe to do the things most pleasing to this growing breed of bipeds.

Next would be the guy with the widest set of eyes who would be the most prolific hunter. The tribe congratulates him, gives him the best women, food and booze. He's the hero.

Then I'd see the author, way below the level of the stage, writing it all down as a historian. I put him there because his name is Maslow. He is low and because mas in Spanish means "more." I put him "more low" than the stage. It works for me because I happen also to speak Spanish. Whatever works for you - use it. Now I have connected a word with the author's name and with an in-mind

movie. I will forever remember the five basic needs and the guy who discovered
it all.

In my Mapping for Memory notes would be the hour's lecture in five
balloons depicting the five major points. [I don't draw balloons well.]

The memory map might look like this:

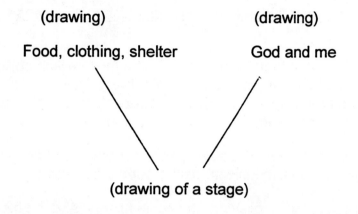

(drawing)   (drawing)

Food, clothing, shelter   God and me

(drawing of a stage)

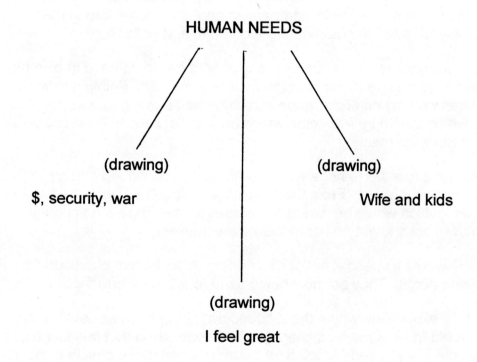

HUMAN NEEDS

(drawing)   (drawing)

$, security, war   Wife and kids

(drawing)

I feel great

(drawing of Lundberg under the stage, pen in hand)

Six months later, I would look at the page and in a few seconds the whole thing would come bouncing back in all it's glory, into full view on my mental movie screen. Instant recall.

BRAINSTORMING IDEAS

2. Capture brainstorming ideas in a manner which makes sense for later analysis.

The other day I sat at a table with the CEO of a multi-million dollar a year company to discuss how he would set up a manufacturing facility in Tijuana and how he would work the financing with an English partner/customer/supplier. This potential partner needed assurances and some kind of agreement.

I took out my notebook, found a blank page, put the book horizontally in front of me and asked him to fill me in with background information.

As he told me about the English company, its history, and the history of the relationship between the CEO's company and the market, I drew green circles. I put the name of the CEO's company in one, drew a red line to the company in England, listed the market share of each, and so forth.

His concern revolved around how many shares he would have to give his English contact in exchange for funding the factory in Mexico. Pointing to words here, shapes there on my notebook page, which he had been following from the first moment, we connected a few items which he had not seen in his months-long analysis before the meeting.

He became excited. He began to think aloud as I continued putting names to pictures we created. From the drawings, he found an angle he had not seen before; one which would be a sure-fire motive for the English company to jump through the hoops to get on board this new venture.

The CEO would not let me out of his building until I let him photocopy the memory mapping notes. They are now being used to launch a new factory.

I can't fully explain the why without sounding like a pseudo-scientist, and instantly you would think of me as a charlatan. All I can say is that this technique works. Every time I have used Mapping for Memory when alone or with a client, things are discovered which should have been seen before. Simple things, obvious things, but they did not stand out until the mapping for memory exercise.

DELIVER THE GOODS

3. Think of, organize and deliver a speech, a sermon, a presentation.

It has been said that some people would rather die than deliver a speech. Would you rather wrestle a crocodile or give a speech at tomorrow's Quality meeting? Invariably the choice is to wrestle a crock.

Why?

It has to do with memory. People freeze when being stared at by a multitude of people. The thought of standing before a group can cause the mind to sink into total panic. All thoughts seem to fly out the window.

If you can learn to deliver a speech without reading it or without fumbling through a stack of cards, which seem always to get out of sequence, you are home free. Mapping for Memory is one of the solutions to the deep freeze. It makes giving a talk so darned easy you will wonder why the world is not filled with speechmakers! It's really fun.

Even if you want to deliver a speech, but don't have the time to visualize a "stage play" or "movie," organize your speech in a traditional way. However, try starting with your paper placed horizontally before you, with the title of the speech in the center with a geometric shape drawn around it. You might double your mental capacity merely with that single act.

Any speech has a beginning, a middle and an end. The beginning usually describes the problem or opportunity. The middle develops the reasons why you will be giving the solution at the end. But it does not mean you have to start thinking and writing your speech in that order.

LOOK TO THE END

I always visualize the end result before doing anything else. To this end result I will build an argument. So on a memory map I will put the end result smack in the upper left corner where people traditionally start their note-taking. It's the first place the eye goes to - we've trained it to do. It's the first word on a piece of paper. It's item number one of a list. It's the headline.

I use the rest of the blank paper to build a series of picture shows so there will be no doubt in my audience's mind that the conclusion is logical and true.

I put a few words for each of these pictures somewhere on the map. Then I start connecting them and crosslinking them, looking for symbols, fewer words and more images, ways to communicate with emotion and feeling.

In my mind's eye I visualize the audience accepting my speech with applause, with them taking out their check-books, signing up for the next session, taking notes to share at work - whatever action I expect as the result of my effort.

When delivering the speech, all I need is a single piece of paper which I can hold, put on a lectern, or project through an overhead transparency. When I conduct a series of lectures to the same group, they eventually learn Mapping for Memory. When I place my own notes on the screen, they easily make it a joint venture of recall and discovery.

When it's all done, I can put the memory map away for an hour, a day, a week or years.

My lecture notebook is filled with mind maps of years ago which I can bring to life instantly with a few minutes of concentration. You see, mental images are like aromas. The faintest hint of baking bread can take us back to grama's kitchen filled with color, cats mew and all the rest. Words simply cannot compete against such awesome power.

INVENTION IS THE MOTHER OF SUCCESS

4. Invent something new. Strategic breakthrough thinking.

Huge companies, bastions of power, industrial giants - all crumble to nothing when they fail to react to changes in their markets.

An outstanding example of this may be when the Swiss watchmakers' research and development scientists told them about quartz. They and shrugged off the information. They didn't even care enough to patent the idea.

We've seen it happen to buggy-whip makers, titans of the slide rule, vacuum tube makers, the telegraph, nylon, memory chips, Apple. And we will continue to see it as we march toward the future.

Change is one the most difficult things to handle - or to accept.

DON'T MESS WITH THE GODS

Cassandra was blessed by Apollo with the ability to see the future, then punished by the same god when he ordered that no one should ever believe her.

People on the front line in many companies, schools, organizations see the change coming their way. They know the poo will hit the fan and they write memos, tell their boss, get newspapers to print their visions - but few people listen.

Time and time again we have seen that if the military top brass would have listened to the soldiers in the field, they would have had time to prepare, to change, to dominate that change and to continue the war.

Not one vacuum tube manufacturer ever got into making transistors. Some people think this a most unusual situation, but we know it happens frequently.

Andy Grove in his book "Only the Paranoid Survive" tells of his own blindness to the changing world and gives thanks to his plant managers and people in the field for having the guts to shift resources into microcomputers even before headquarters became aware of the changes taking place. This is an unusual story. It is unique.

BE THE INNOVATOR

In today's ever changing world those who can create strategic breakthroughs are the companies which will continue to grow, to survive, to provide increased wealth and well-being to country, customer and employee.

The student who can prove he has the tools to achieve strategic breakthroughs will never have to worry about not having a job. The person on a career path will be assured of having a brag sheet filled with examples of how he instigated major change resulting in huge profits or huge savings. That kind of resume gets jobs.

So what has strategic breakthrough thinking have to do with Mapping for Memory? Let's solve a problem.

PROBLEM SOLVING

5. Problem solving alone or in a group.

I was invited to meet with a director at Solar Turbines, a division of Caterpillar, to see if I had any ideas on solving a nasty problem which related to making jet engine combustors. The finished combustors had worked well for two years. Then, suddenly, they had gone out of control. Nearly every combustor failed to pass a burn-in test.

For six months their best people had tried to unravel the problem with no success. The problem was getting worse.

They put me to work to find the cause and a solution.

My first picture was that of a burning combustor.

For three days I went to every person who had anything to do with the combustor. I interviewed the original design team, the supervisors on the assembly line, the technicians at the test rig, and every one in-between. I took notes and questioned everything. It was easy to do after I told them I knew absolutely nothing about jet engines or combustors. Of course they wondered why the company would hire a person who didn't know the business. But that's what management does, and they shrugged it off and gave me the answers I needed.

The fourth and fifth days were Saturday and Sunday. I spent them walking about my garden, taking naps, jotting notes, dreaming, deep breathing and walking some more. I looked up every reference in my library on the subject, went back into thermodynamics, into some basic physics, and simply filled my brain with information. My notebook was filling with pictures and diagrams, yet I hadn't a clue.

I was putting a lot of pressure on memory as I kept visualizing the pictures and diagrams I had drawn.

Monday I was back at the test rig brainstorming with the technicians. I wanted to see a test, to feel the heat, to put my hand on the test device and feel the throbbing power of jet fuel being ignited making the power of a thousand horses flow through a small opening. I had to get inside the flame and be a part of it. I drew a picture of myself inside.

We talked some more.

On Tuesday I let my mind roam, to become a part of the fireball inside the combustor.

I could feel the inconel walls, the flow of air through the cooling vanes, the spray of jet fuel being ignited by the row of spark plugs, the blast of air coming in under pressure of the vanes, the super-hot exhaust gases nearly melting the power turbine blades (which was the problem).

I could see the temperature sensors at the outlet and could almost feel them near the point of melting and knew it was wrong, wrong, wrong.

A RUSH OF COLD AIR

From back in high school days, I then remembered myself under the hood of my car. I recalled the car engine as we crossed over high mountain passes and how it would overheat even in the cool air. Lean - it was running lean. I drew the car and a red line from it to the turbine blades. Were they running lean?

Back to the rig. I asked for the last reject to be put back for test. But first I requested they cover 20% of the front air inlet holes with something. Tack weld some shims or plug them somehow. They did it. We ran the test.

IT WORKS!

As the sensor temperatures appeared on the screen, we saw them in the normal range. When the final printout appeared, the unit had passed exactly in accordance to specifications. What had happened?

We now knew the fuel mixture was the cause of the problem but not the reason. Nothing in the manufacturing process had changed. I drew the holes, and it hit me like a ton of bricks. They had tightened the quality control on the size of the holes.

I went to engineering and asked how they had determined tolerances. They said the new laser was incapable of making close-tolerance holes, so they had run some formulas based on the randomness of the Yag laser drill, which cut by trepanning, and specified hole diameter accordingly.

I asked what would happen if every hole were made to plus or minus three thousandths instead of the actual capability of the laser, which was over five. They said the flow would be out of balance.

NEVER MESS WITH HOLES

That was it! When the first unit failed at test, the quality people measured holes against drawing specifications and found them to be all over the place. So they started reaming laser pierced holes. Which changed the design configuration. Which resulted in a fireball under greater front air pressure than it should be. Which made the fireball touch the rear vanes and caused the combustor to be a reject.

WHAT DID I DO?

Okay, let's see if you got all my thinking processes and all the scenes in the right order. Listen, think, research, analyze, test idea through imagination, press for inspiration, expect inspiration, test inspirational ideas, explore alternatives, test again if need be, develop hypothesis, validate, test again.

Throughout, I was drawing pictures, connecting lines, <u>and visualizing the pictures in my mind</u>.

Repeat process until I achieve success.

SO WHY THE MEMORY?

Where is memory in all of this long story? At all times, bits and pieces of information from a zillion places are in motion. Without being able to see how they interrelate through pictures, how they push and pull each other, there is simply no way to handle all the information.

In summary, Mapping for Memory not only betters your memory, it improves your thinking processes. It works in tandem or synergistically with the other memory methods set out in this book. It is an important tool for the solution of problems.

Footnotes:

1. Wayne Lundberg is a problem solver and inventor. Among his many inventions are a meatball making machine capable of putting a dozen one inch in diameter meatballs into cans of spaghetti at the rate of 36,000 per hour; a hand-held metal condition analyzer used to determine the material condition of sheet metal before it goes into the drop-hammer, which thus can predict the results; a six station rotary queue to automatically load and unload two-ton palettes of pre-assembled inconel components into and out of a vacuum brazing oven; and a self-contained shop built on barges and placed at strategic locations around the world for Caterpillar to deliver spare parts within 12 hours through the use of satellite transmitted CAD.

2. "Eureka, I have found it!" proclaimed Archimedes shortly after laying peacefully in a warm bath and observing the level of water rise and fall with his breathing. The king had challenged him to find a way to tell if the gold crown the king had bought was 100% gold, or if it contained air pockets or other material, such as lead. The water displaced by the crown would yield the exact volume of the crown, which could then be compared with the weight of that same volume of gold.

3. They and their fellow impressionists were thrown out. They had to exhibit their art in a special place for the `refused'. Thus the name, Salon des Refuses.

If you haven't found the time to memorize the Numerical Order Alphabet, it is suggested that you order the four audiocassettes. You can listen to them as you drive to work, and it will be a piece of cake. See the information on the last page of this book.

CHAPTER TWELVE

OTHER ALPHABET CUE SYSTEMS

My wife has a terrible memory. She
remembers everything.

In Chapter One I emphasized that memory was dependent on associations, and to recall an item, it had to be associated with something in your consciousness. Next, you learned the Numerical Order Alphabet, which allows you to hook images of items you want to remember to pictures of key words in the alphabet which you have memorized.

The key words of the Numerical Order Alphabet were determined by using a Transposing Code in which consonants represented the digits from zero to 9. Using these consonants, key words were chosen to represent the numbers from 1 to 200.

Even if you forgot one of the key words, it was easy to recall it, since phonetically you knew what the word had to sound like: 71 had to sound like cat, cot or cut and 52 had to sound like lane, line, lean or loan.

Once the Numerical Order Alphabet is learned and retained in memory, it becomes easy to attach unrelated items to it for recall.

Now I can show you alternate specialized alphabets for hooking or linking which require little effort to learn.

Remember, though, the Numerical Order Alphabet has an advantage over all other alphabets and linking methods - you can instantly recall the numerical position of any item in the list without counting from the first item.

HABLA INGLES?

One of the simplest alphabets is the ENGLISH ALPHABET. I first mentioned using it at the end of Chapter Three. It is so easy to use as a cue system, it deserves repeating.

I can't tell you how many times the English Alphabet has assisted me in remembering a name. I see the face, either actually or in my mind, and I can't recall the name. I start going through the alphabet, starting with A, and more times than not, when I get to the letter corresponding to the first letter of the person's name, I have the feeling that it is right. If the name doesn't come to mind, I add a vowel to see if the letter and the vowel together make the association for me. I am amazed at the number of times I have been successful using this technique, and I have used this alphabet to bring to mind many items other than names.

WE GOT HOOKED

We also have learned the Hook Method, the grand daddy of all the artificial methods used to assist memory. It was to the parts of a house that the ancient mnemonists hooked the information they wanted to remember. We've worked extensively with this method throughout this book.

The basic weakness of the Hook Method is that the hooked items remain only briefly in short-term memory due to displacement, fading and lack of logical relationships between unconnected items.

When we have frequent need for a hooking device to recall unconnected items, we developed alternate alphabets to avoid the process of displacement.

Another reason for having alternate alphabets at your tongue tip is that the alphabet should be totally different from the items you want to hook to it. If you need to describe a medical physical examination, you wouldn't want to use the BODY PARTS ALPHABET (Chapter Ten). If you are a clothing salesperson, you would not want to use the DRESSING ALPHABET, coming next.

GET DRESSED

One of the shortest alphabets is the DRESSING ALPHABET. A businessman usually puts his clothes on in the order of shorts, socks, shirt, slacks, shoes, tie and jacket. If he wants to remember certain items to bring to the office or to the football game on the next day, he can associate those items with his articles of clothing. When he starts dressing, he will remember the item he associated with his shorts, socks and so on. Women could have a longer list if they add the acts of applying make-up to their list of clothing.

THERE ARE JUST SEVEN

If you want DAYS OF THE WEEK ALPHABET, just chose an object you would associate with each of the seven days. At times, I have used the words of my Dressing Alphabet to represent the days. Monday is shorts, Tuesday socks, and so on with shirt, slacks, shoes, tie and jacket. I use Monday as the first day of my week, as I have always considered Saturday and Sunday as the weekEND.

If you want remember dates and appointments, the Days of the Week Alphabet works well.

For example: Monday I speak to the Riverside Ladies' Golf Association. I could visualize golf balls in my shorts. Tuesday, I will put on a hypnosis show in New York. I could envision the Empire State Building in my socks.

THERE ARE ONLY TWELVE

A little longer alphabet is the MONTHS ALPHABET, which allows for twelve hooks. Just associate as your key word for each month some object which you normally associate with the month. My list of key words is as follows:

January	Skis
February	Valentine
March	Marching soldiers
April	Showers
May	Flowers
June	Bride
July	Firecracker
August	Beach Ball
September	Laborer
October	Pumpkin

November   Turkey

December   Santa Claus

For example: Any major events that will occur in January, which you wish to remember, you will hook to the picture of skis. If there are a number of events, link the events and then hook them to the picture of skis.

IS A HIPPOPOTAMUS BETTER THAN A HAMSTER?

Depends on how big your house is.

For up to 26 hooks, I like the ANIMALS ALPHABET. It is composed of one animal for each letter of the English Alphabet. As I start through the English Alphabet from the letter A, the animal whose name begins with that letter instantly pops into my mind. If I have hooked an item to that animal, I will recall the item when I envision the animal. Here is the Animals Alphabet.

A   Alligator

B   Bear

C   Cat

D   Dog

E   Elephant

F   Fox

G   Giraffe

H   Hippopotamus

I   Iguana

J   Jaguar

K   Kangaroo

L   Lion

M   Mouse

N   Newt Salamander

O   Ostrich (bird)

P   Porcupine

Q   Quail (bird)

R   Rabbit

S   Skunk

T   Tiger

U   Urchin (marine animal)

V   Vampire bat (bird)

W   Wolf

X   Xanthus (Achilles' horse)

Y   Yak

Z   Zebra

I had to stretch a little to match a few letters, but it works. Although these animals are not in a numbered order, the great advantage of the Numerical Order Alphabet, it's pretty easy to zip through the English Alphabet to get to any of the animals.

The true determinant of when you have the list memorized will be when you can name the animals in order without thinking of the letters of the English Alphabet.

OTHER SPECIALIZED ALPHABETS BASED ON THE ENGLISH ALPHABET

The Animals Alphabet is just one example of the many specialized alphabets which can be devised to be based on the English Alphabet, with one key word for each of the twenty-six letters.

A horticulturist might develop alphabets related to fruits, flowers or vegetables.

A forest service ranger might develop an alphabet related to trees.

A hardware store salesman might develop an alphabet based on tools.

If you will review all the alphabets described in this book, please notice I have tried not to include the same object in more than one alphabet.

ACRONYMS

A very simple cue system is the use of acronyms - words formed from the first letters or syllables of other words.

UNESCO is derived from United Nations Educational, Scientific, and Cultural Organization. Hardly anyone would remember the full name of this organization without knowing the acronym.

Didn't AT&T derive from Atlantic Telephone and Telegraph Company? GM from General Motors?

When you read the Contents of "The Complete Book of Home Welding," did you notice the author used three acronyms? GMAW represents gas metal arc welding. SMAW represents shielded metal arc welding. FCAW represents flux-cored arc welding. If you want to design a memorable sentence to associate all three acronyms, you could take the first two letters of each acronym and say, "General Motors makes small, fine cars because of their welding." [The latter is an acrostic. It is the reverse of an acronym in that we have made a phrase with each letter being the first letter or the second letter of each word in the phrase].

Open your newspaper and glance at the symbols for stocks listed on the New York Stock Exchange. Many of them are acronyms.

Listen to the television or radio. Listen to your own conversations. You probably hear or use a number of acronyms every day of your life.

In summary, acronyms are useful when we want to refer to or recall with ease the names of organizations or titles - in many cases by using a well-known acronym it will not be necessary to spell out the name of the organization or the full title.

CHAPTER THIRTEEN

YOUR HOUSE, HOME STREET AND HOME TOWN ALPHABETS

An inexperienced speaker arose in confusion
after dinner and murmured hesitantly:

"My friends, when I got here only God and I
knew what I was going to say to you, and now only
God knows."

Let's take a look at a few alphabets which are not based on numbers or the letters of the English Alphabet. They might be a little more difficult to construct, but for the person who needs many alphabets, they may come in handy.

WHAT'S IN YOUR HOUSE?

Think of all the things you are familiar with which might serve as hooks. What about furniture? If you pictured yourself entering your house and seeing each item of furniture as you walk from room to room, you would have your HOUSE ALPHABET.

I don't take credit for this alphabet - remember, it was Simonides, the famous Greek orator, who conceived of it around 500 B.C. Following his day, this alphabet was the primary aid for all mnemonists for over two centuries. Something about it must have been good.

The House Alphabet finally was replaced by early forms of the Numerical Order Alphabet in the 1800's.

The following list is comprised of some of the articles of furniture or equipment you might see as you walk from your living room to the kitchen.

sofa

chair

bookcase

telephone

television

piano

bench

fireplace

andirons

lamp

picture

door

carpet

refrigerator

dishwasher

table

oven

toaster

coffee maker

microwave

mixer

(If Simonides had had toasters and microwaves in his day, his speeches could have been longer.)

You can add as many rooms as you wish.

Since you should have no problem remembering the order of the furniture and equipment, merely hook an item you want to recall to each. Good for short lists and when you do not want to overwork your other alphabets.

WHAT'S ON YOUR HOME STREET?

What about your neighborhood? You go in and out of your house every day. Even if you never took the time to observe your street, you can't help but be at least vaguely familiar with it.

I hadn't seen the street where I grew up for about 25 years. When I went back to Lima, Ohio for the 50th reunion of my high school class, I went back to see it. The block looked pretty close in 1998 to how it looked when I lived there in the 1940s. I could never forget it because the repetition of the sight of it every day then and the occasional fond thought of it through the years kept it in my long-term memory.

If I want to remember a number of unrelated objects or concepts, I can just hook them to locations on my HOME STREET ALPHABET.

I took photos of the houses on the street to make sure that their distinguishing features would not fade from my memory. Using an external aid to memory is an acceptable tool.

I'll briefly mention some of the memories the houses brought to my mind as I walked up and down the street.

I started with the Jean Court, where I often rode my bike around the circle. Jack lived in the first house on the court. He shot me with a beebee gun when I rode my bike on his lawn. I frequently climbed the rock post at the end of the Jean Court property. Still on top was the handle I cemented over 50 years ago to make climbing up it easier. Next came the Elm View Court. Ronnie and Jimmie Gross lived in the first apartment. Becky lived in the next one. On her porch I copped my first breast feel. The rear of the Elm View Court faced my house. Becky always undressed with the shade up.

My father bought our house in 1936 for $3,300.00 when he was earning $25.00/week. The Meredith's lived next door. Virginia Meredith was in my class. She kept her shade down.

A cop lived next door to them. I never rode my bike on his lawn, but at the next house I dumped a can of garbage on the porch on Halloween. They called the cop.

Around the corner were two duplexes. Dick Dillon lived in one. We were good friends. At the end of the block, facing Lowell Grade School, was

Matthew's Drug Store. It is out of business now, but I spent a lot of time at the soda fountain. Henry Guggenheimer lived next door to it.

I used to mow the lawn of the corner house across the street from mine for 25 cents. They were rich. The Alexanders lived directly across the street. She was the friendliest person on the block. Jelly-belly Gladys lived next to them. I always wanted a beebee gun to deflate her when she swung on her porch swing.

Reverend Baker and his daughter, Heidi, lived next to Gladys. I thought they were German spies. On the porch of the house next to the spies, I learned to play Monopoly. I didn't go near the far house on the corner because twice I knocked out the side window with baseballs.

You can see how easy it is for me to attach objects to various parts of each of these houses. The Home Street Alphabet is deeply imbedded in my memory.

I start with the Jean Court and work my way down my side of the street and then up the other side. It would be impossible for me to forget one of these cue pictures.

If you move around often and don't have a home street firmly in mind, you can utilize important landmarks of your city.

IT'S PRONOUNCED "lime-uh"

Here is my HOME TOWN ALPHABET for Lima, Ohio. With the exception of the new public library and the elementary school, all the structures were in existence in 1947, the year I went to college.

1. Lima Memorial Hospital, where my first hernia was repaired.

2. The football stadium where Lima Central and Lima South played out their great rivalry.

3. The track in the stadium where I ran the high hurdles.

4. The EDCO sign where my brother-in-law's business burned to the ground.

5. The First National Bank Building on the Town Square.

6. The City Loan Building. The Meredith brothers had their law office in it.

7. The Kewpee hamburger stand. It was the heart and soul of my adolescence.

8. The Trinity Methodist Church where Boy Scout Troop Six met and I became an Eagle Scout.

9. The West Ohio Gas Company. It never blew up.

10. Goodyear, where I filled my bike's tires with air, and the blimp never landed.

11. The synagogue where my sister, Muriel, married Ralph Edelman.

12. The Shell station where I gassed up my 1932 two-door Ford with rumble seat when I drove home from college.

13. The museum. I contributed 25 cents for its construction when I was in the first grade.

14. The new public library. One of my father's paintings hung in the old library.

15. The YWCA. I never got inside it.

16. My sister's house on Market Street.

17. The County Court House. Fortunately, I never got inside it, either.

18. The War Memorial Building. Thank God I was too young to be drafted.

19. The YMCA where I danced with Gerry Bowsher in the Y-teen club. I danced with her again at my 50th high school reunion.

20. Lowell Elementary School. It was built after I wrecked the old one.

21. The playground where I spent many a happy recess until Dean Stearns beat me up.

22. The house my father designed and had built just before I left for college.

23. The temple across the street from our new house.

24. Woodlawn cemetery. I never met anyone there whom I knew.

25. The lake in Faurot Park where I caught many a crawdad.
    It's a wonder I can eat lobster now.

26. The summer arts and crafts building in Faurot Park where I
    became the checkers champion of Lima at age six.   [Also
    the jacks champion.]

To link these structures, I made a simple street map and followed it in my mind when I wanted to remember the pictures and their hooks in the proper order.

HOMEWORK

It's time for you to design your own house, street and town alphabets.

Take out your sheet of paper and make a list of all the major articles of furniture and equipment as you go through your house. This will be your own House Alphabet.

Did you do it?

Okay, take a look outside at your home street. Take a good look. There will be things you never noticed before. It's because you are now doing more than seeing. You are observing. If you have moved, take the time to go back to where you grew up. Walk the street. Now you have your own Home Street Alphabet and probably a lot of restored good memories.

Designing your Home Town Alphabet will be a little more difficult. You will have to do some brain work. It's not easy recalling all the prominent structures in your town. You'll have to get out and take a drive.

While you are at it, take pictures of your street and the prominent structures of your town. Over the years, these structures will change. But you'll want to maintain and refresh your memories.

There you have it. Three nearly instant alternate alphabets to work with.

CHAPTER FOURTEEN

DATES AND APPOINTMENTS

Storekeeper: "Well, hello, Adam Walsh. I met you in Bozeman five and a half years ago at your company's exhibit at the Gallatin Gateway Inn. You were with your wife, Betty. She wore that pretty blue dress.

Salesman: "Goodbye, sir."

Storekeeper: "Aren't you going to sell me something?"

Salesman: "No. I sell memory training courses."

With the invention of personal digital assistants, or PDAs - small hand-held devices for keeping appointments, addresses and things-to-do lists - people are relying less on their memories to remember important dates or appointments.

If you are a salesman on the road and you have a multitude of appointments every day, PDAs are invaluable aids. But if you need to remember only a few dates or appointments, it would be better if you relied upon your memory.

Two reasons:

1) Use it or lose it. If you don't stress your memory, it will become less efficient.

2) If it becomes apparent to your business associates, customers or friends that you can remember dates, they will consider you to be intelligent and your opinions to be important.

And it is easy.

I'VE GOT A DATE

For an important date in the future, picture in your mind something which reminds you of the date.

For example: If you are taking a friend to see "Phantom of the Opera," picture the face mask. To the mask, hook the key word for the month from our Months Alphabet. If the month is December, you could have Santa Claus wearing the mask. For the day of the month, hook the key word from either the primary Numerical Order Alphabet or from the secondary. For the 22nd, you could chose "noon" or "nun." How about having a nun sitting on the lap of a masked Santa Claus? Two hooks and you have it. You could even go to the Dictionary of Word/Number Conversions for additional picture words for the 22nd day.

My wife's birthday is June 3rd. At first I had trouble remembering if it was the sixth or the third. Now I picture a birthday cake in my mind. Immediately hooked to it I see a bride (June) cutting a ham on top of the cake (number three from the secondary Numerical Order Alphabet representing the 3rd day of the month).

I'm not going to wait until the sixth anymore to give Helen her birthday gifts.

For appointments you want to keep during the week, you need to remember only the day of the week and the hour.

For the day of the week, you can use the Dressing Alphabet or seven other picture words you want to represent the seven days. I prefer substituting the key words of the Dressing Alphabet.

For example: I have an appointment for Tuesday at 9:15 A.M. with my tailor. I might picture him darning a pair of socks (Tuesday). To that combination I will hook the hour.

If I can remember the hour using a cue system, the time within the hour should pop up by itself. So for 9:15, I need only use a key word for 9. My choices from the Numerical Order Alphabets are "bay" and "hoop." I'll picture my tailor sitting in a basketball hoop, darning my socks.

WHAT TIME IS IT?

If you have many appointments you want to commit to memory, you might find you are overusing the key words from the Numerical Order Alphabets. You have a choice of designing a new alphabet to represent time. It's a lot more work, but if you find you frequently will use it, it might be worth the effort.

You could go to the *Dictionary of Word/Number Conversions* and choose twenty four words which are not in the primary or the secondary Numerical Order Alphabet. Ignoring the first zero, how about these for the TIME ALPHABET?

01:00	-	Hood
02:00	-	Inn
03:00	-	Hem
04:00	-	Row
05:00	-	Wheel
06:00	-	Witch
07:00	-	Cow
08:00	-	Foe
09:00	-	Boa
10:00	-	Dice
11:00	-	Toad
12:00	-	Dane
13:00	-	Dome
14:00	-	Tire
15:00	-	Tool
16:00	-	Ditch
17:00	-	Dock
18:00	-	Thief
19:00	-	Tub
20:00	-	Wines
21:00	-	Nut
22:00	-	Onion
23:00	-	Enema

24:00   -   Norway

If you don't care to use the 24-hour military system of stating time, you can stick with A.M. and P.M. hours. Even though the hours are duplicated, it shouldn't be confusing. If you have a 10:00 appointment with your doctor, you know it won't be at night. It would have to be in the A.M. The primary disadvantage is having twelve less picture words at your disposal to use for hooks.

Oh, come on, Doc, how many alphabets do I have to learn? I heard you say it.

I didn't say you had to commit them all to memory right now, especially this optional one for the hours. But you'll see, it won't be too difficult to do the job over a period of several weeks. You will be amazed when you've learned every alphabet in this book within... let's say at least one month, if you repeat them every day. And it doesn't take more than fifteen minutes to go through every one of them.

BACK TO TIME

You have the hour and the day picture words for making associations. Put them together. On Monday morning you review your important appointments for the week. What objects have you hooked together?

As for me, I visualize my shorts with the hearts pattern in the jaws of a Great Dane dog (12:00). Holding the dog by a leash is my accountant. Ah, ha. I have a Monday noon luncheon appointment with my accountant.

I used two hooks to associate the appointment with my accountant.

ANOTHER WAY

You knew from previous chapters that I was going to make it easier, didn't you? [It's pretty difficult for you to know that I am teaching you the best methods, if I don't show them all to you].

You have a number of appointments for Monday. You don't want to use your shorts over and over again, as it might get confusing. You don't want to learn the Time Alphabet. Also, you'd rather rely on one hook instead of two (the shorts and the Dane).

Then give each day of the week a number. Monday would be 1, Tuesday 2, Wednesday 3, Thursday 4, Friday 5, Saturday 6 and Sunday 7. Combine the number with the hour of the appointment. You end up with only one object to hook to the person you are meeting.

For example: You know you have an appointment with your dermatologist next week, but you want to be sure of the day and time. Picture him in your mind. You see him with tattooed arms, so you know your appointment is for Monday at 11:00 A.M.

How did you do it?

For the noon appointment you combined 1 (Monday) with 11:00 (the hour). The appointment number became 111. From the *Dictionary of Word/Number Conversions* you had your choice of the words:

dated, edited, tattooed, dotted and deadwood.

All these represent the number 111. When you made the appointment with the dermatologist, you chose <u>tattooed</u> and pictured him with tattooed arms.

The Dictionary has a variety of picture words for each three-digit number. By varying the words you choose, you'll avoid overuse of the same key words. And, by using three-digit numbers, you need to make only one hooking association.

PRACTICE, PRACTICE, PRACTICE

Grab your pen and paper. Using the Months Alphabet from Chapter Thirteen and the secondary Numerical Order Alphabet, make associations for the following important events:

Speech seminar	-	July 5th
Cruise to Hawaii	-	May 22nd
Pay your Income Tax	-	April 15th
Your parents' anniversary	-	November 21st
Your boss's anniversary	-	August 7th
Divorce trial	-	October 4th
Bankruptcy lawyer	-	October 6th

Using numbers for the days of the week and the *Dictionary of Word/Number Conversions*, make associations for these appointments:

Orthodontist	-	Wednesday 3:00
Attorney	-	Friday 10:00
Car dealer	-	Thursday 7:15
Audition	-	Wednesday 12:00
Sales seminar	-	Tuesday 8:30

Remember, you shouldn't need to make associations for parts of hours.

in Appendix D you can compare your associations with those I made.

CHAPTER FIFTEEN

PICTURE WORDS, LINKS AND THE NUMERICAL ORDER ALPHABET

Of iniquity, we are a din.
There's so much sex, it's a sin.
They're always going at it,
and, frankly, I've had it!
I just don't remember when.

Dennis Taylor

A brief summary. We developed the Hook Method and utilized the Numerical Order Alphabet as a cue system to provide two sets of hooks, each containing 100 picture words. This is the method of choice when we need to know the numerical order of things. We also have designed alternate cue system alphabets.

In Chapter Three, we developed Fantasy Images of peoples' exaggerated features and attached the images to Picture Word substitutes for their names. The resulting combinations we called "Ringers."

In Chapter Eight, linking of longer numbers was introduced. Long numbers were converted into words and then linked together in sentence or story form.

In Chapter Nine we saw how ideas can be reduced by summarization and outlining into cue words. These were then linked together into a story.

Hooking and linking, linking and hooking.

Not yet demonstrated is the combinations of picture word substitutes for names, hooking, linking and the Numerical Order Alphabet. Of course, that is what I'm going to do next.

LET'S SUPPOSE

What if we need to remember a series of events or a list of people in chronological or numerical order? We can attach to the Numerical Order Alphabet a combination of picture word substitutes and links. In some cases we can hook the substitutes to the Numerical Order Alphabet without needing any links.

This technique can be applied to types of information such as: battles, books of the bible, buildings, discoveries and inventions, eminent and remarkable people, heads of countries, and treaties.

For example: Let's see how the technique of combining picture word substitutes for names, links and the Numerical Order Alphabet applies to Presidents of the United States.

As of 1998, there have been 42 presidents. We'll use the first 42 key words in the secondary Numerical Order Alphabet. We could just as easily use the first 42 key words in the primary Numerical Order Alphabet, but I like to spread the wealth around.

Once we have the Presidents listed, we choose picture words to represent each of their last names.

If we can't visualize a good picture word, then we develop a linking sentence.

Before we do the list, think back to the English Alphabet. If you will recall, often just going through the English Alphabet can jog a memory to recall the name of a person. If you feel a certain letter feels right, but the name doesn't pop up, you can add a vowel to the letter to see if the combination brings up the name. It's remarkable what thinking of one or two English alphabet letters can do.

WHAT IF WE HAD THREE?

If we establish word pictures or links which utilize the first three or more letters of a name, recalling the entire name should be slam dunk. That's how I wrote my mnemonic for the Presidents of the United States.

Here it is, using the secondary Numerical Order Alphabet.

1. Washington - A dish<u>wash</u>er in the hut.

   (The dishwasher is the picture word substitute for
   Washington and it is hooked to the hut, which represents
   the first President)

2. Adams - A hen on <u>a dam</u>

   (hooked)

3. Jefferson - The <u>chef</u> slices the ham.

   (hooked; this is the rare case where I had to use
   a rhymer)

4. Madison - The hare in the trap is <u>mad</u>.

   (linked)

5. Monroe - A hole full of <u>mon</u>ey.

   (hooked)

6. Adams - <u>A dam</u> on either side of a hedge.

   (hooked)

7. Jackson - A car <u>jack</u> on a hook.

   (double hooked)

8. Van Buren - A hoof sticking out of a <u>van</u> door.

   (hooked)

9. Harrison - A <u>hairy</u> hoop.

   (hooked)

10. Tyler - A daisy growing out of a <u>tile</u>.

    (hooked)

11. Polk - <u>Poke</u> the deed through the hole.

    (linked)

12. Taylor - A <u>tailor</u> sewing in the den.

    (hooked)

13. Fillmore - <u>Fill more</u> of the dam.

    (linked)

14. Pierce - An arrow <u>pierc</u>ing the deer.

    (linked/hooked)

15. Buchanan - The dial in a <u>buck</u>et.

    (hooked)

16. Lincoln - A dish on top of <u>Lincoln</u> logs.

    (hooked)

17. Johnson - A duck sitting on the <u>john</u>.

    (hooked)

18. Grant - A dove perched on <u>granite</u>.

    (hooked)

19. Hayes - The dip spills on the <u>hay</u>.

    (hooked)

20. Garfield - The noose tight around a bag of <u>gar</u>bage.

    (hooked)

21. Arthur - A nude with a big he<u>art</u>.

    (hooked)

22. Cleveland - <u>Cleave</u> the nun in half.

    (linked)

23. Harrison - A <u>hairy</u> man doesn't freeze in Nome.

    (linked)

24. Cleveland - The winner crosses the line in <u>Cleveland</u>.

   (linked)

25. McKinley - Mt. <u>McKinley</u> in the Nile.

   (hooked)

26. Roosevelt - A notched white <u>rose</u>.

   (hooked)

27. Taft - A box of <u>taffy</u> in the nook.

   (hooked)

28. Wilson - The knife sliced the <u>will</u> in half.

   (hooked/linked)

29. Harding - He broke his tooth nipping the <u>hard</u> candy.

   (linked)

30. Coolidge - The moose on the ice is <u>cool</u>.

   (hooked/linked)

31. Hoover - The maid pushes the <u>Hoover</u> vacuum.

   (hooked/linked)

32. Roosevelt - Two pink <u>rose</u>s on the moon.

   (hooked)

33. Truman - The mummy is a <u>true</u> dead <u>man</u>.

   (linked)

34. Eisenhower - <u>Ice on</u> the mare.

   (hooked)

35. Kennedy - Mule in a dog <u>kenn</u>el.

   (hooked)

36. Johnson - Mesh covering two <u>johns</u>.

    (hooked)

37. Nixon - Mug with <u>Nixon</u>'s mug.

    (hooked)

38. Ford - A movie showing a Model-T <u>Ford</u>.

    (linked)

39. Carter - <u>Cart</u> loaded with mops.

    (hooked)

40. Reagan - A <u>ray gun</u> shoots a red rose.

    (hooked)

41. Bush - A rod sticking out of a <u>bush</u>.

    (hooked)

42. Clinton - <u>Clean</u> a <u>ton</u> of dirty ruins.

    (linked)

43. _____

(I leave this one to you)

Take ten and memorize the list. You'll be surprised how quickly you can do it.

When you have the list down pat, have your spouse or a friend name any President. You'll give his numbered position. Have them give you a number from 1 to 42. You'll name the President. Then find your fifth grade teacher and show her how smart you are.

CHAPTER SIXTEEN

MEMORY GAMES

Waiter, an hour ago I ordered a steak. Have you
forgotten it or have I eaten it?

Memorizing playing cards has been a standard for stage mentalists and amateur mnemonists for a very long time. There are several variations in vogue: 1) the performer can describe in what order each of the cards has been drawn 2) the performer can report which cards were not drawn, and 3) the performer can tell which cards were drawn and which cards were not drawn for each of the four suits.

Since the first variation requires knowing in which order each card was drawn, the Numerical Order Alphabet is the best cue system to use.

We need to decide whether we want to use the key words from the primary or secondary list, or whether we should start a tertiary list. To refresh your memory, here are the complete primary and secondary lists:

1. Tea	Hut	35. Mail	Mule	68. Chef	Chief
2. Noah	Hen	36. Match	Mesh	69. Chip	Chop
3. May	Ham	37. Mike	Mug	70. Case	Kiss
4. Ray	Hare	38. Muff	Movie	71. Cat	cot
5. Law	Hole	39. Map	Mop	72. Can	Cone
6. Jaw	Hedge	40. Race	Rose	73. Cam	Comb
7. Key	Hook	41. Rat	Rod	74. Car	Crow

8. Fee	Hoof	42. Rain	Ruin	75. Coal	Coil
9. Bay	Hoop	43. Ram	Room	76. Cash	Couch
10. Toes	Daisy	44. Rear	Rower	77. Cake	Coke
11. Tot	Deed	45. Rail	Reel	78. Cuff	Calf
12. Tan	Den	46. Rash	Roach	79. Cap	Cape
13. Tam	Dam	47. Rake	Rock	80. Face	Fuse
14. Tar	Deer	48. Reef	Roof	81. Fat	Foot
15. Tail	Dial	49. Rope	Rabbi	82. Fan	Phone
16. Tissue	Dish	50. Lace	Lasso	83. Fame	Foam
17. Tack	Duck	51. Lot	Lid	84. Fare	Fur
18. Taffy	Dove	52. Lane	Lion	85. Fall	File
19. Tap	Dip	53. Lime	Lamb	86. Fish	Fudge
20. Nose	Noose	54. Lair	Lure	87. Fig	Fog
21. Net	Nude	55. Lily	Lilli	88. Fife	Five
22. Noon	Nun	56. Lash	Leech	89. Fob	FAB
23. Name	Nome	57. Lake	Lock	90. Base	Pass
24. Nero	Winner	58. Leaf	Loaf	91. Bat	Pot
25. Nail	Nile	59. Lap	Lip	92. Bean	Pan
26. Niche	Notch	60. Chase	Cheese	93. Beam	Palm
27. Neck	Nook	61. Chat	Sheet	94. Bar	Pear
28. Navy	Knife	62. Chain	Shin	95. Ball	Pail
29. Nap	Nip	63. Chime	Jam	96. Badge	Peach
30. Mass	Moose	64. Chair	Shore	97. Back	Peg
31. Mat	Maid	65. Chile	Shell	98. Beef	Puff
32. Man	Moon	66. Judge	Choo-choo	99. Baby	Pope

33. Mama	Mummy	67. Check	Chick	100. Thesis	Disease
34. Mare	Mare				

In a deck of playing cards there are four suits of 13 cards each. We will need four groups of key words to represent the suits of Spades, Hearts, Diamonds and Clubs. To minimize the process of displacement, we should choose key words which we use infrequently for other memory needs. To avoid having to memorize yet another list of key words (except for spades), let's work with the secondary list.

To help in differentiating the suits we can precede the number of the playing card with the first letter of each suit - S for spades, H for hearts, D for diamonds and C for clubs. We'll consider these letters to be neutral or silent, so they will not be transposed into a number.

WHAT IS BLACK AND WHITE AND LIES ON A TABLE?

For the suit of spades we can't take our key words from the primary or secondary Numerical Order Alphabets because none of key words start with an s. We'll use:

(Ace) 1. Seat (s is neutral; t transposes to 1)

2. Sun

3. Seam

4. Sewer

5. Sail

6. Sash

7. Sack

8. Safe

9. Soap

10. Seeds

How would you picture these key words?

If you were sitting face to face with me, you would tell me that they should be black because spades are black. Right! What else? They could be made bizarre, enlarged, multiplied and given some action. Right again.

So, take paper and pencil. Draw the pictures which are easiest for you to remember.

Oh, you're trying to catch me now - I forgot the Jack, Queen and King. Ah, but I was saving those. How do we represent them?

Just about every mnemonist who has memorized and written about playing cards visualizes picture words for eleven, twelve and thirteen.

I say "Why?" Why make up a substitute picture when these cards already are pictures? All I do is picture the Jack standing up holding a shovel (a spade), the Queen lying on a chaise lounge with a shovel across her lap, and the King on the throne with a shovel stuck into his crown.

THE OTHER THREE SUITS

Hearts, diamonds and clubs have words in the secondary Numerical Order Alphabet starting with h, d and c. Since these key words are used infrequently, we can use the following list:

	Hearts	Diamonds	Clubs
(Ace) 1.	Hut	Deed	Cot
2.	Hen	Den	Cone
3.	Ham	Dam	Comb
4.	Hare	Deer	Crow
5.	Hole	Dial	Coal
6.	Hedge	Dish	Couch
7.	Hook	Duck	Coke
8.	Hoof	Dove	Calf
9.	Hoop	Dip	Cape
10.	Hats	Dots	Cats

New words were chosen for the ten of each suit.

Hearts and diamonds in red. Clubs in black.

Here is how I visualize the picture cards:

Jacks: Jack digging with a spade

                Jack standing on a beating heart

                Jack with a diamond-shaped crotch

                Jack holding a club like a bat

Queens: Queen with a spade handle in her mouth

                Queen with a large beating heart

                Queen with a huge diamond ring

                Queen clubbing a watermelon

Kings :   Large spade on his crown

                Large heart on his crown

                Large diamond on his crown

                Large club on his crown

The only new key-word list is for spades, and you just have to add the four new key words for the ten of each suit.   I'll give you ten minutes to commit the spades and tens to memory.

CARD PLAYING - FIRST VARIATION

Have someone in the audience or at a party shuffle the deck, draw and call out all the cards, one by one. Have another person write each card, as it is called out, in order on a chalkboard pre-numbered from 1 to 52. Without you looking at the chalkboard, have the audience call out the name of any playing card. You will tell them its numerical position. You can also state which card is on either side of the named card.

Or reverse, have them call out any number between 1 and 52. You will tell them the card located at that numerical position.

How do you do it? Simple.

You will use the first 52 key words of the primary Numerical Order Alphabet for your hooks. To each of these key words, hook the pictures of the cards drawn, in sequence. Since the key words for the tens and the spades are new and the key words for the other three suits come from the secondary Numerical Order Alphabet, there will be no duplication.

You can even do it blindfolded!

Of course, you don't need to go to extremes and have them draw out all 52 cards. 15 or 20 certainly would prove the point.

Here's an example.

The first ten cards drawn out are the (1) ace of hearts, (2) ten of hearts, (3) eight of clubs, (4) four of clubs, (5) jack of spades, (6) two of diamonds, (7) three of spades, (8) ten of spades, (9) seven of diamonds and (10) king of hearts.

You could make the hook associations like this:

1) On a red <u>hut</u> place a huge cup of tea.

2) Place several red <u>hats</u> on Noah's head.

3) Picture a black <u>calf</u> standing above and urinating on the May page of a calendar.

4) See a <u>crow</u> standing in a ray of light.

5) See the <u>jack of spades</u> shoveling dirt in front of a lawman.

6) See a fox's jaw sticking out of its red <u>den</u>.

7) Picture a key unlocking a <u>seam</u> on a black shirt.

8) See a pile of red <u>seeds</u> on the counter as you pay your fee.

9) It's a red <u>duck</u> swimming in the bay.

10) It's a red <u>king of hearts</u> staring at his huge toes.

You would continue and hook the rest of the drawn cards to your Numerical Order Alphabet.

PLAYING CARDS - SECOND VARIATION

Have a person randomly draw 15 cards from the deck and write them on the chalkboard out of your sight. Have someone else draw and call out the remaining 37 cards. You then tell the audience which 15 cards were written on the chalkboard.

This is easier than the first variation because you don't need to know the order in which the cards were drawn. Since you don't need to know the order, you don't need to use the Hook Method and the Numerical Order Alphabet.

As the remaining 37 cards are drawn and called out, you can either mentally tear in half the word pictures representing those cards; in your mind run a red line diagonally across them; envision each one hooked to the same object, such as a table, a waterfall, a fire - anything; mutate them; or color them green or any other color.

When all the 37 cards have been drawn and called out, think through your four suits of picture words. Those 15 cards which don't have changes made to their basic pictures are the ones written on the board.

It only requires recognition to play this game.

Here is an example:

Assume the same ten cards we listed in Variation One are the first ten of the 37 cards called out.

They were (1) the ace of hearts, (2) ten of hearts, (3) eight of clubs, (4) four of clubs, (5) jack of spades, (6) two of diamonds, (7) three of spades, (8) ten of spades, (9) seven of diamonds and (10) king of hearts.

If you wanted to imagine throwing a can of blue paint on all of them, you could visualize them as follows:

Blue paint running down the roof of the red <u>hut</u>.

Two <u>hats</u>: one blue and one red.

A black <u>calf</u> standing with one foot in a bucket of blue paint.

A <u>crow</u> floating on a pond of blue paint

The <u>jack of spades</u> shoveling blue paint.

Blue paint pouring out of the red <u>den</u>.

Blue paint seeping out of a <u>seam</u> on a black shirt.

Red <u>seeds</u> floating on top of a bowl of blue soup.

A red <u>duck</u> swimming in the blue bay.

The red <u>king of hearts</u> with a blue heart.

You would similarly continue with the remaining 27 yet undrawn and uncalled out cards.

When all the 37 cards have been read to you (15 cards having been written on the chalkboard previously) you would mentally review all the cards in the deck, starting with the ace of spades and working upwards through that suit. As you come to the three, ten and jack of spades, you would see the distorted pictures made of them and would know that those cards were not written on the board. Any spade not mentally distorted would be one of the 15 cards written on the chalk board, and you would list them for the audience.

Continue the same way with the other three suits.

PLAYING CARDS - THIRD VARIATION

This is the one I use frequently when on stage. It's quite similar to the second variation and almost its reverse. No chalkboard is required. Instead of a member of the audience calling out the 37 cards remaining after the first 15 are drawn out and written on the board, he will say aloud the first 15 drawn cards and set them aside. I will mentally disfigure or change the word pictures of each of the 15 cards.

The remaining 37 cards will then be distributed by the person still holding them to four other members of the audience, each one getting only one suit. One gets the spades, one the hearts, one the diamonds and the last one the clubs. I then have each of the four people put the cards in numerical order.

Next, I have each of the four people, one at a time, stand and hold up his cards, fanned out, without showing them to me. I mentally run through each person's suit, starting with the ace. Those cards which are distorted are part of the missing 15.

For example: I will say, "You have the ace, two and three of hearts. You are missing the four of hearts. You hold the six, seven and eight of hearts but are missing the nine..."

When I have performed this with all four people, I will have identified all 15 missing cards. Voila!

The Third Variation is easier than the Second Variation, since I only have to go through the process of distorting and remembering 15 cards instead of 37.

I suggest you go through your suits in the same order. I prefer spades, hearts, diamonds and clubs - the same order of value as they are given in the game of Bridge.

Another nice feature of memorizing playing cards is that since a deck of cards is small, you can carry one with you and practice during free moments.

You might also occasionally use this method of remembering cards when playing a card game. But you should reserve it for special hands. It would be very difficult to use it with more than several hands without your associations becoming mixed up, even if you used a different type of distortion each time.

Other variations of remembering playing cards have been proposed, such as using a linking method to associate the cards in sentences or to picture the cards attached to parts of your own body. I find these methods to be much more difficult than the methods you have just learned.

Go buy a deck of cards and start practicing.

WHAT'S MY NAME? GAME

Cut out photos from magazines and paste each on a separate sheet of white paper. Write a fictitious name beneath each picture and five brief details about the person, such as occupation, age, marital status, hobbies, sports, college, favorite football or baseball team.

Have everyone sit around in a circle. Pass a sheet to each one. Every twenty seconds, ring a bell and have them pass their sheet to the next person. When they have seen all the sheets, gather them up.

One by one, flash the sheets, the name and description covered up, and have your guests write down the name of the person they see. Winner gets a prize.

For tie breakers, see how many items of description can be recalled.

You also can do this by teams.

I find this is a very good game to play by participants during the interactive segment of a memory improvement seminar.

WORD PICTURES

From your Roledex Picture-Word File, put a single word picture on a large card. On the back side, write the name. Divide your guests at a party into two teams. Show the word picture to one team and see if they can guess the name the picture represents. Give the team one minute to guess the name. Then show another word picture to the other team. The winning team is the one which gets the most correct answers.

What's nice about this game, it keeps refreshing your memory with your word pictures. But don't tell your friends you had an ulterior motive in playing this game.

CHAPTER SEVENTEEN

MEMORY DISTORTION

At Wellesley, Vassar, and Smith,
A common and recurring myth,
That a masculine member,
Helps students remember,
Was found without substance or pith.

Memory can be <u>distorted</u> in a number of ways. In Chapter Two I
mentioned that memories can be changed through expansion and reconstruction.
In addition, memories are subject to distortion through suggestion, imagination
and hypnosis.

FILLING IN THE GAPS

When part of a memory is lost, or there is a gap in what was perceived,
the mind tends to fill in the blank with something else which seems logical to it,
even if the padding is untrue. This the expansion of memory through "rounding
out" is an ongoing process occurring daily by our subconscious minds.

For example: A bank is being robbed. The customers in the bank drop to
the floor as shots are fired at the robbers.

The customers might be able to describe what the robbers looked like,
that guards were in the bank, that shots were fired at the robbers, and that the
robbers ran. Who shot at the robbers would be significant testimony But the
customers didn't see who fired the shots. Many witnesses' subconscious minds
would fill in the gap, making them believe they actually saw the guards pull out

their guns and fire. This belief would be logical. However, it would be untrue, since an off-duty policeman did the shooting.

Another example: A woman might remember having a 16th birthday party but not recall blowing out the cake candles because more important to her was her interaction with the boys attending the party. Years later, when later asked about the party by her children, and realizing she must have blown the candles out, her subconscious mind might construct a false image for that occurrence, which image would be accepted by her as true. She might recall her mother standing next to her when she blew them out, but her mother actually might have been in the kitchen scooping ice cream at that moment.

Third example: You look around your house for your car keys. You finally find them beneath a dining room chair. When you had arrived home earlier, the phone was ringing. In your dash to answer it, you flung the keys on the chair. Unseen by you, your dog knocked the keys off the chair. Since only the ringing phone was important to you, what you did with your keys never entered your short-term memory. If your spouse asks you how your keys got under the chair, you wouldn't remember what you actually did with them, but your subconscious mind might construct a logical, but untrue, image for you - that you flung them on the floor as you ran to the phone.

If you will accept the proposition that 99% of the events of our lives either never enter our short-term memory or they have faded from our long-term memory, [what did you do all day last Tuesday or ten Tuesdays ago?] then it is easy to conclude that there are great gaps in our memories which are subject to being filled in (padded) under certain circumstances, such as stress or interrogation.

I SHOOT NO BLANKS

What if we remember an event for which there is no gap of memory, but over time what we remember about it becomes distorted? How does that occur?

Distortion of events recalled can occur naturally through the process called reconstruction. Each time you recall an event, new associations or bits of information are added and some facts are lost. You might tell a friend about your school days or your Las Vegas vacation, but it won't be exactly the same story you told to someone previously. New information or twists will be added to the story, and they become part of your memory.

I SUGGEST YOU LOVED EVERY PAGE OF THIS BOOK

Changes in your memory can also be brought about by suggestion.

A number of psychologists and researchers have proved that false memories may be implanted in a significant percentage of people by mere suggestion. If that false memory is suggested at a subsequent session, an increased number of people will recall it as being a true memory.

One of the experiments to prove this involved suggesting to individuals that they saw certain events during their first day after birth - true events being impossible to recall due to the immature nature of the brain at that time. The false memories were implanted either through a waking age regression technique or through hypnotic age-regression. A majority of the subjects in both groups recalled the false memories.

How many times has a relative or friend mused to you over past events of which you have only a hazy recollection? That person might have had a distorted memory of the events, but the description seemed logical to your mind. You might very well have accepted it as having occurred. It now is part of your memory.

IMAGINATION

If a person, without suggestion from others, imagines events occurring in the past that did not occur, those imaginations also can become part of memory and be recalled as being true events. Day dreams [wishful dreams while you are awake] about the future may help to set goals, but day dreams about the past may distort true memories.

We should be aware that suggestions and imagination can create "memories" of events which did not actually occur. If we avoid being subject to suggestions about our past and we don't engage in wishful thinking as we recall past events, our memories will retain more validity.

There have been recent court cases where patients have accused psychiatrists of implanting false memories - usually related to abnormal sex acts or being sexually assaulted - during treatment sessions. The misinformation was fed to the patients by their psychiatrists either by hypnosis or by other suggestive techniques. An excellent article on this is CREATING FALSE MEMORIES, Elizabeth F. Loftus, in Scientific American, pages 70-75, September, 1997.

LOOK INTO MY EYES

One of the most effective ways to change memories is through the use of hypnosis. As part of my hypnosis stage shows, I often have constructively used suggestion to change subjects' habits. Distinct from the planting of false sexual memories by the psychiatrists in the court cases, when I use suggestion to change habits, it is at the request of the subjects and with their full waking knowledge that I intended to implant false memories to help them diet or stop smoking.

To cause a patient to abstain from overeating, a false memory of being allergic to certain foods can be implanted. Who is going to want to eat chocolate if his mind is filled with events where he became deathly ill from eating it - perhaps was hospitalized and had his stomach pumped?

Implanting false memories is not the only hypnotic technique utilized. The patient needs to be motivated to eat less or to exercise more. By hypnotic suggestion, the subject might visualize being in a play in which he is slender and the object of everyone's attention and affection because of his build. By suggestion, he might be made to feel pride at being slender. He might be made to see himself in a better job or to be married to a beautiful woman.

These are but a few of the hypnotic techniques which can be utilized synergistically to achieve the goal of losing weight.

Likewise, the hypnotic implantation of false memories can be utilized to change a person's character or characteristics.

The purpose of this book is not to detail the many uses of hypnosis through memory distortion, but to give you an idea as to how it is done.

But what about hypnosis and your remembering events or information which you want to recall? How can hypnosis help you?

LOOK INTO YOUR OWN EYES

First, you have to be capable of self hypnosis, since you are not going to run to a hypnotist every time you want to remember something.

How does one become a good hypnotic subject.

The easiest way is to have a hypnotist place you into the hypnotic trance state. Then the hypnotist could give you a posthypnotic suggestion such as:

Whenever you want to become hypnotized and enter this wonderful state where you can control your own self, just put your right hand on your left shoulder and say your name three times. You immediately will be hypnotized, but you will have complete control over your trance. When you want to awaken yourself from the trance, just put your left hand to your forehead and say awaken, and you will awaken.

While hypnotized, you will be able to suggest to yourself that you will concentrate on whatever you want to study or learn and not be disturbed. You will be able to suggest to yourself that you will remember everything you read while you are hypnotized. You will be able to suggest to yourself that you will use a memory system and that you will remember the important points of your study.

You will be able to suggest to yourself that you will feel much better and be better off by memorizing the material.

Each time you enter the hypnotic state, you will find that it is easier the next time to be hypnotized and your concentration and memory will improve each time.

I am now going to awaken you. After you are awake, you will put your right hand on your left shoulder and say your name three times. You immediately will be hypnotized and you will then suggest to yourself that whenever you want to study and learn under hypnosis, you will hypnotize yourself.

(If I were to hypnotize you, I would add that you will tell everyone you know how great this book is and that they should run out and buy it and the four memory improvement teaching tapes that make learning much easier.)

If you have ever attended an hypnosis stage show, you might have seen the hypnotist <u>regress</u> subjects back to earlier years. If you have ever been in hypnotherapy with a psychiatrist, you have experienced regression. In both cases, events are relived which the subject or patient had truly forgotten. But the events still remained in a part of memory that was not recoverable by ordinary means.

These "forgotten" memories may have been determined to be irrelevant by the recall selector cells, which prevent such information from reaching the conscious mind. They may have been intentionally blocked from retrieval because they were of events which the psyche didn't want to remember.

In any case, because through hypnotism the suggestions reach directly into the subconsciousness, bypassing selector cells or blocking cells, it is possible to retrieve these memories.

One still needs to be careful in evaluation of such memories because memories are active and are not accurate recordings of past events due to distortion by expansion, reconstruction, imagination and suggestion.

My neighbor once told me that if my memory systems didn't do me no
good, I should write them down.

CHAPTER EIGHTEEN

TELEPHONE NUMBERS

When I was young and couldn't remember girls' names,
I was clever and would ask the girl whether she
spelled her last name with an i or an e. This
worked well until I met Martha Hill.

To better understand why the memory system I will be demonstrating is the best way to remember phone numbers, a review of the history of phone number mnemonics is in order.

(You know I will end with the easiest system for you).

The early mnemonists had it very easy. Since telephones had not been invented, they had no need to devise a memory system for their phone numbers. Cute, huh?

Bruno Furst in 1948 illustrated a method for remembering numbers in his book "Stop Forgetting" He used his publisher's phone number - Plaza 9-1450.

Applying a linking method, he formed a word from the first two letters of the name of the exchange (Plaza) and the exchange number (9). Then he found words which converted from each of the sets of two digits (14 and 50) of the trunk line which could logically link in phrase form to the first word. The finished product was:

Plaza 9 - 14   50

Playboy author illustration.

If he was unable to combine the exchange and the exchange number into one word, he broke them up into two words, such as:

<u>Pl</u>easant <u>b</u>ooks <u>th</u>oroughly i<u>ll</u>us<u>t</u>rated.

Furst did not, however, consider linking or hooking the phrase to "Greenberg," the name of his publisher. To make a better association, he could have made the sentence read:

The green playboy author illustrates.

or

The green pleasant books thoroughly illustrated.

In his 1951 book "Three Weeks to a Better Memory," Brendan Byrne suggested visualizing the telephone exchanges, such as:

<u>Telephone Exchange</u>	<u>Visualization</u>
Whitehall	A white hall
Oregon	Map of Oregon
Plaza	Hotel Plaza

The difficulty of his method was that Byrne was forced to use the same picture words over and over when many of the numbers he wanted to memorize were in the same exchange. This would lead to confusion. Furst could use any word which started with the first two letters of the exchange, so he could vary the phrases.

Byrne was not a good prognosticator. Area codes were introduced in 1951, and on November 10, 1951 the first public direct-dial long distance call was made. By the early 1960s, the entire country was hooked up. Telephone exchange names were a thing of the past.

Byrne also suggested finding picture words for numbers of four and five digits. But if one attempts to write a word/number dictionary, as I have done, it quickly becomes apparent there is great difficulty in finding words which can convert to numbers of four or more digits.

Byrne also recognized this problem. He then proposed making a sentence out of the Numerical Order Alphabet letter representing each digit. For example: An exchange and trunk line number of

6 - 6   4   5   1

he converted to

<u>G</u>eorge <u>g</u>ave he<u>r</u> he<u>ll</u> <u>t</u>oo.

If he added the word representing the name of the exchange, Byrne would end up with a phrase or a sentence consisting of six words. Furst only needed three or four words to do the same job. Byrne should have read Furst's book. Today, he would have even more difficulty because of the longer telephone numbers.

CAN YOU HOOK A NUMBER?

In his book "How to Develop a Super Power Memory," Harry Lorayne in 1957 proposed hooking together picture words which represented the sets of digits.

> "Let's say that you wanted to remember that Mr. Silverberg's phone number was JU 6-9950. You might "see" a picture of a shiny silver iceberg sitting in a courtroom as a judge (JU 6) smoking a gigantic pipe that's covered with lace!"

Lorayne also divided the trunk line into two sets of two digits: 99 = pipe and 50 = lace. He did recognize the need to tie the phone number to Mr. Silverberg. The problem with his proposal was that it was difficult to determine which came first - the pipe or the lace. He called it his "fly in the ointment." His proposal required the use of three picture words to be hooked up to the picture words representing the name of the person. This is not easy to do.

In our illustration of the Hook Method in Chapter Six, we only had to hook one picture word to each key word in the Numerical Order Alphabet key. Further, there is a disadvantage with a Hook Method - you can only use picture words, and there a lot fewer of them than when you use a linking system, where all words can work.

Check out the *Dictionary of Word/Number Conversions* in Appendix E to compare the number of picture words to all the words which represent any number.

To reduce the number of hooks, Lorayne suggested using only one word to represent all four digits of the trunk line. But we know how difficult it is to find 4-digit words.

HE TAUGHT THE IMPOSSIBLE

Today, with our longer phone numbers, the use of a hook system is a near impossibility. I'll show why.

The following is an illustration from Bob Burg's "The Memory System," published in 1992. He calls it a chain link method, but it is the same series of hooks Lorayne used 35 years earlier. Only in 1992 there were three additional digits in a phone number.

"The next telephone number you need to remember belongs to your accountant, Bruce Strauss; it is 215-5332. In beginning your Chain Link, you could use an adding machine to remind you that this number is for your accountant. In this case, however, he is also a friend, so you want to lock in his number by way of his name. The name Strauss itself does not present a mental picture, does it? Let's use the Soundalike mouse. That sounds enough like Strauss to remind you of his true name, doesn't it? For the prefix 215, you can use noodle (nu, duh and luh). Of course, you could also use natal, needle or anything else that would fit... The next step is to remember the four numbers, lime (53) and moon (32). Now, associate mouse with noodle. See this mouse sneaking his way into a bowl of noodles. In fact, there is one noodle that looks particularly good. You feel the mouse needs to add something to make the noodle taste even better. That's right, some lime (53). See this mouse squirting a sour-tasting lime on that noodle. Now, wanting true dining atmosphere, our squeaky hero goes outside, taking with him this noodle sprayed with lime so he can eat it under the moon (32) light. Bruce Strauss' telephone number is 215-5332."

Isn't that enough to make you vomit? What sane person would ever go through that mumbo jumbo (339 639) to recall a phone number? And, Burg did not even integrate the area code into his chain link!

PATIENCE IS A VIRTUE

Okay, you've been waiting patiently for me to reveal the Amazing Method to Recall Phone Numbers. It's really not brilliant, but it is simple and it works.

Let me refresh your memory. In Chapter Eight I described how to link longer numbers. I gave you an example of how to recall all the powers of two up to the 64th power.

The 64th power of two is:

18446744073709551616

That's 20 digits I easily can recall. As I mentioned, I broke the number down into groups of two and three digits:

18 446 744 073 709 551 616

Then, using my *Dictionary of Word/Number Conversions*, I quickly converted the numbers to a linking sentence for the words representing the 20 digits and hooked/linked them to chair (64). I ended up with a sentence which I memorized through several repetitions:

> 64. The chair thief re-register's career and schemes to explain loyalty in a hugeditch.

Well, if it is easy to recall a number containing 20 digits hooked to an object, or to a name, then a phone number containing only 10 digits hooked/linked to a name should be child's play.

Example: John Adams phone number is 213-965-0705.

> I see it as 213 965 07 05.

I go to the *Dictionary of Word/Number Conversions* and note which words are available for these four sets of numbers. To save you the effort of flipping back and forth to Appendix E, I'll list them here.

213   anthem, entomb, indemnity, nightmare, nutmeg, ointment.

965   bushel, bachelor, pugilist.

07   sack, seek, sock, sky, ask, husk, soak, whiskey.

05   sale, sail, slow, solo, Sally, Saul, swell, zeal.

In seconds I am able to make up some memorable sentences, such as:

Adams' nutmeg bushel soaks a seal.

In Adams' nightmare a pugilist socks Sally.

Adams entombs the bachelor in a sack of swill.

Voila! Repeat any of the phrases a few times, and I've got Adams' number.

If necessary, I could even hook any of the linking phrases to a vision of Adams with a large Adams Apple.

I didn't even look at all the words I could have substituted for the two-digit sets - those words with more than two consonants.

For example: Since you would know to use only the first two sounds of a word for each of the trunk line sets of two digits, for the digits 07 you could also use any of the 53 words in the dictionary representing the numbers from 070 to 079. For the digits 05, you could additionally use any of the 47 words representing the numbers from 050 to 059. Just look at all the possible combinations of words available to form a memorable sentence to recall Adams' phone number.

So don't confuse me with any other phone number system you may have stumbled across. My mind is made up. Right or wrong, I'm going to stay with my method.

For those few of you who find recalling phone numbers is still difficult, don't give up the faith. By the year 2025, when America is due to run out of area code numbers, advances in voice recognition technology may well make remembering numbers a thing of the past. You'll just speak into a phone from anywhere in the country. It will recognize your voice, locate the person you name in your personal on-line phonics phone book, and connect to that person.

But what are you going to do until then?

CHAPTER NINETEEN

WHAT DID YOU LEARN?

A policeman noticed a 92-year-old man crying on a park bench, and he asked why he was so sad. "I just got married to a 23-year-old woman who makes love to me three times a day." "Then why are you crying?" the policeman asked. "A man of your years should be very happy." That's not why I am crying," the old man answered. "I can't remember where I live."

Ron Langill

I hope you learned a helluva lot. I spent weeks writing this book. I even had some very good friends edit it for me.

Did you start a Life Experience's Notebook? Did you take the first step toward preserving your personal address and phone books or Rolodex's?

As you worked your way through the chapters, did you take notes? Did you organize the material by summarizing, outlining and classifying?

Well, after I wrote this book, I went back to see what I did. I explained the following concepts:

CONCEPTS

Association

Concentration

Cue systems

Cue words

Displacement

Distortion

Encoding

Expansion

Fading

Interference

Key words

Memory

Observation

Organization

Recall

Reconstruction

Registering

Regression

Retention

Suggestion

Transposing Code

I hope you can explain each term in one or two sentences. If not, go back to square one.

Are you familiar with the types of memory?

MEMORY TYPES

Immediate/working/ultra short-term

Recent/short-term

Remote/permanent/long-term

Episodic

Semantic

Implicit

>How about the methods of enhancement that I enumerated?

ENHANCEMENT METHODS

Action

All Senses

Amplification

Exaggeration

Multiplication

Replacement

Transformation

Zany Pose

>Do you recall the laws of nature?

LAWS OF NATURE

Similarity

Contrast

Propinquity

>Or a sub-classification of the Laws of Nature?

Rhymers (soundalikes)

Synonyms

Neighboring

Matching Pairs

Antonyms/Opposites

Cause and Effect

Whole and Part

General and Specific (genus and species)

Phrase links

      Recall the memory methods. If you've forgotten, I'm coming to get you.

MEMORY METHODS

Acronyms

Acrostics

Association

Classification

Fantasy images

Hooking

Hypnosis

Jingles

Linking

Mapping for Memory

Organization

Outlining

Picture words/Word pictures

Repetition

Ringers

Suggestion

Summarization

Verses/poems

      And, of course, the alphabets.

ALPHABETS

Animals Alphabet

Body Parts Alphabet

Days of the Week Alphabet

Dressing Alphabet

English Alphabet

Home Street Alphabet

Home Town Alphabet

House Alphabet

Months Alphabet

Numerical Order Alphabet

Time Alphabet

For those of you willing to take the time to write:

EXTERNAL MEMORY AIDS

Meetings Notebook

Picture-Word File

Life's Experiences Notebook

There I did it. I said I wasn't going to outline or classify for you, but I have a good heart. I just want you to know it all and to live by it. Every day and in every way I want you to practice what I have preached and what you have learned.

IF ALL ELSE FAILS

I have exhausted my mind teaching you what I know to be the best ways to improve your memory. If you gained nothing from this treatise, there still is hope for you. I can prescribe a memory ointment, a powder or a pill for you.

You'll have to admit Aristotle was brilliant. He strengthened his memory with this ointment:

> "Take the fat of Moles, Bears if it be to be had, of Weesel and Bever, or instead of that of Otter, of each an equal quantity; Juice of Betony, add Rosemary; of all which make an Ointment to anoint the Temples, chiefly in cold weather."

Marius D'Assigny, 1706

How about this pill?

> "Take Cubebs, Calamint, Nutmegs, Cloves, of each a Dram and a half; the best Frankincense, choice Myrrh, oriental Ambergrise, of each a Scruple and a half; Mosch, five Grains: with Marjoram-water make Pills. Take one in going to Bed, and two at Sun-rising, five hours before Meat; in the Winter every Month, in the Spring and Fall more seldom."

Thanks also to Marius.

If you take one, wait until morning before calling me.

APPENDIX A

VEHICLES ORGANIZATION AND CLASSIFICATION

A man went to the doctor one day
was told he had cancer, but hey
you won't regret it
for you will forget it
'cause you also have Alzheimer's I'd say.

Edward Carroll

Here again are the vehicles I listed for you.

Nissan King Cab

Dodge Caravan

GMC Suburban

Cadillac Seville

Ford Escort

Chevy Malibu

Plymouth Voyager

Toyota 4Runner

Infinity sedan

Mercedes sedan

Chevy Silverado

Ford Explorer

Toyota Camry

Chevy Astro

Ford Ranger

Land Rover

Ford Winstar

Toyota Tacoma

Hyndai Accent

One way of classifying them is by whether they are manufactured by a foreign or a domestic company.

Domestic	Foreign
Dodge Caravan	Nissan King Cab
GMC Suburban	Toyota 4Runner
Cadillac Seville	Infinity
Ford Escort	Mercedes
Chevy Malibu	Toyota Camry
Plymouth Voyager	Land Rover
Chevy Silverado	Toyota Tacoma
Ford Explorer	Hyundai Accent
Chevy Astro	
Ford Ranger	
Ford Winstar	

You could also classify them by type of vehicle.

Sedan	Pickup	Van
Ford Escort	Nissan King Cab	GMC Suburban
Chevy Malibu	Ford Ranger	Plymouth Voyager
Toyota Camry	Toyota Tacoma	Chevy Astro
Infinity	Chevy Silverado	Ford Winstar
Mercedes		
Cadillac Seville		Sport Utility
Honda Civic		Dodge Caravan
Hyundai Accent		Toyota 4Runner
		Ford Explorer
		Land Rover

Another way would be by price.

High	Medium	Low
GMC Suburban	Dodge Caravan	Nissan King Cab
Cadillac Seville	Chevy Malibu	Ford Escort
Infinity	Plymouth Voyager	Ford Ranger
Mercedes	Toyota 4Runner	Toyota Tacoma
Land Rover	Chevy Silverado	Hyundai Accent
	Ford Explorer	
	Toyota Camry	
	Chevy Astro	
	Ford Winstar	

Another classification could be by manufacturer: General Motors, Toyota, Ford, etc.

If you have a long list of vehicles, you could sub-divide them by type of vehicle and then sub-classify them by either price or by domestic or foreign manufacturer.

APPENDIX B

CHECKOFF CHART OF OUTSTANDING FEATURES

There was an old man of Khartoum
Who kept two tame sheep in his room
to remind him, he said,
of two friends who were dead;
But he could not remember of whom.

Dean Inge

THE HEAD

Rectangular

Round

Square

Egg shaped

THE HAIR

Wavy

Curly

Crew Cut

Parted

Straight

Receding

Pigtail

Buzz cut

Bowl cut

HAIR COLOR

Blonde

Brown

Black

Grey

Red

THE FACE

Round

Square

Oval

Broad

Long

Location of wrinkles

Cheek bones

THE EARS

Small

Large

Lobes - long, short or absent

THE FOREHEAD

High

Low

Narrow

Wide

Bulging

Receding

THE EYEBROWS

Bushy

Arched

Straight

Thin

Meeting

Separated

THE EYES

Bulging

Small

Asian

Large

THE NOSE

Pointed

Concave

Convex

Straight

Flat

Pug

BASE OF NOSE

Up turned

Down turned

Horizontal

THE LIPS

Full

Thin

Large

Small

Protruding

SPACE BETWEEN UPPER LIP AND NOSE

Long

Short

THE CHIN

Pointed

Square

Cleft

Jutting

Receding

Double

ADORNMENTS

In hair

Ear rings

Nose rings

Glasses

APPENDIX C

LIST OF PICTURE WORDS AND PHRASE LINKS FROM CHAPTER THREE

I remember putting it right there.
It couldn't have vanished in thin air.
Well, I'll just grab my specs
and then...oh, heck!
I know I had them right here somewhere.

Dennis Taylor

PICTURE WORDS

Abalos   - abalone, Appaloosa, Apollos

Abbott   - a butt

Abdullah   - a dull H

Abell   - bell; ape ball

Abernathy   - a natty bear

Abraham   - a brown ham

Abrams   - abrasions; a broom

Abrego   - a brig

Acevedo   - saves dough

Aceves   - a sevens; ace vase

Ackerman   - Akron man; hacker man

Acosta	- ascot
Adame	- a dame; a dam
Addison	- adder sun; daddy's son
Adkins	- dad's kings
Agopian	- egg opener
Aguilar	- guitar; uglier
Aiken	- aching
Akopyan	- copying
Alarcon	- a lark on
Alas	- a lass; Alice (of Wonderland)
Alba	- Albany; albatross
Albert	- Alberta
Alcala	- alkaline; alfalfa; alcazar
Alcantara	- a cantor; cantata
Alcaraz	- Alcatraz
Aldana	- all Danes
Alejo	- alehouse
Aleman	- beer man
Alex	- elixir
Alfaro	- pharaoh
Alfonso	- phones
Alford	- fort; Ford
Allen	- allen wrench; alien
Allison	- liaison
Alonso	- loons

Alpert   - Alberta

Alston   - stone

Altman   - old man

Alvarado   - avocado

FIRST NAMES FOR PHRASE LINKING WITH A LAST NAME

Beth   - Matt

Bobbie   - Sox

Chester   - Drawers

Doris   - Ajarr

Earl   - E. Byrd

Eugene   - Splitter

Frank   - Wiener

Gerrie   - Atrik

Grant   - Malone

Harold   - Man

Helen   - Wheels

Howard   - Udoit

Jack   - N. Jill

Karen   - Shop

Lane   - Inwait

Philip   - Up

Robin   - Banks

Roland   - Hay

Ryan   - Wheat

Ruth — Less

Sam — Beau

Selma — Carr

Susan — Wins

Wallace — Tumblyn Downe

PHRASE LINKING WITH A FAMOUS LAST NAME

Alan — Greenspan

Dwight — Eisenhower

Emerson — Fittipaldi

Eva — Peron

Evander — Holifield

Fidel — Castro

George — Bush

Gloria — Allred

Imelda — Marcos

Leonardo — da Vinci

Maria — Shriver

Mario — Cuomo

Michael — Jordan

Noel — Coward

Olympia — Dukakis

Paula — Prentiss

Rene — Russo

Richard — Nixon

Rush   - Limbaugh

Salvador   - Dali

Sylvia   - Sydney

Teresa   - Wright

Woody   - Allen

I have a neighbor who never does what he was supposed to do. He always has an explanation - he never heard about it. Maybe he heard about it, but he doesn't know who told him. All he knows is that he remembers something, but he doesn't know what he remembers. But he does remember that he should have remembered something. The only thing he really knows he remembers is that he forgot.

Jackie Mason

APPENDIX D

PICTURE WORDS FOR DATES AND APPOINTMENTS

"I raised to my lips a spoonful of the tea in which I had soaked a morsel of cake...And suddenly the memory returns. The taste was that of the little crumb of madeleine which on Sunday mornings at Combray...my aunt Leonie used to give me, dipping it first in her own cup of real or of lime-flower tea."

Marcel Proust, 1913

This is how I would have you remember the dates and appointments listed in the test at the end of Chapter Fourteen.

Speech seminar   -   July 5th

As you listen to a speech, a <u>firecracker</u> sits in a <u>hole</u> in floor in front of you.

Cruise to Hawaii   -   May 22nd

A <u>nun</u> stands on the bow of the cruise ship holding a bouquet of <u>flowers</u>

Pay your Income Tax   -   April 15th

You're standing in the rain <u>shower</u> by a sun <u>dial</u> paying my income tax.

Your parents' anniversary   -   November 21st

A <u>nude</u> hands a <u>turkey</u> to your parents on their anniversary.

Your boss's anniversary   -   August 7th

You open your boss's door with a <u>key</u> and hand him a <u>beach ball</u> on his anniversary.

Divorce trial   -   October 4th

You hand the judge a <u>pumpkin</u> and your wife a <u>hare</u> at your divorce trial.

Bankruptcy lawyer   -   October 6th

The bankruptcy lawyer drops a <u>pumpkin</u> on your head as you lie in the <u>hedge</u>.

Appointments:

Orthodontist   -   Wednesday 3:00

33 = A <u>mummy</u> and the dentist are pulling your teeth.

Attorney   -   Friday 10:00

510 = The attorney is eating <u>lettuce</u> as you sign the bankruptcy papers.

Car dealer   -   Thursday 7:15

47 = The car dealer smashes your car with a <u>rake</u>.

Audition   -   Wednesday 12:00

311 = You portray a <u>maiden</u> in a Shakespeare play at your audition.

Sales seminar   -   Tuesday 8:30

28 = You demonstrate putting a <u>knife</u> to the neck of potential customer at your sales seminar.

APPENDIX E

Dictionary of Word/Number Conversions

There was a young fellow named Puttenham,
Whose tool caught in doors upon shuttin"em.
He said, "Well, perchance
it would help to wear pants,
If I could just remember to button `em."

Tony Davie

This dictionary includes only a sampling of words which can be converted to numbers. I have listed the words most well known to me. If you need to make a conversion and can't find a fitting word from this list, go to your Webster's. Where two words have been used for a number, I tried to find combinations which have some semblance of a relationship between them.

It is not necessary only to use words from the English dictionary. You may use slang words, foreign words or even make-up words which can convey a meaning to you. You can even misspell words, if you desire. I am sure I have. Remember, when you convert numbers to words, they are merely symbols of meaning and will be for your use only. Use whichever symbols give assistance to your memory.

The diagram of the Numerical Order Alphabet is repeated here.

0	1	2	3	4	5	6	7	8	9
s	t	n	m	r	l	sh	k	f	b
z	th					ch	q	v	p
soft c	d					j	ng	ph	
						soft g	hard g		
						hard c			

For the rules of use, please refer to Chapter Four. For numbers with one or two digits, I generally listed words with an equal number of phonetic consonants. For numbers with three digits, I found words with an unlimited number of phonetic consonants. Just use the first three phonetically sounding letters of each of these words.

00   size, seize, sauce, oasis, Suez, saws.

001 sister, cyst, Sistine, society, assessed, zest.

01   city, soda, stew, sad, acid, sat, cite, stew.

002 sizeness, socinian, Susan, assassin, season.

02   sane, seen, sun, snow, sign, scene, soon, swan.

003 sysymbrium, Sesame.

03   same, seem, sum, swim, sewer, Siam.

004 size roll, siserary, Caesar, Cicero, saucer.

04   seer, sour, sore, zero, sir, sower, czar.

005 sizzle, sizel, scissel, sossle, Sicily.

05   sale, sail, slow, solo, Sally, Saul, swell, zeal.

006   SOS channel, a wise sage.

06   sage, siege, such, sash, usage.

007   sizing, siskin, seasick, seizing.

07   sack, seek, sock, sky, ask, husk, soak, whiskey.

008   sassafras, Sisyphean, Sisyphus, suasive.

08   save, safe, sofa, sieve, salve, Sophia.

009   sizable, sizably, sea soup.

09   sap, soap, soup, sob, sip, asp, hasp, swipe, wasp.

010   citizen, seduce, sideways, South sea, cities, sides.

011   state, stout, statue, steady, ceded, estate, wasted.

012   stain, stone, satin, sadden, Sweden, stun, sudden.

013   stamp, stump, steam, stem, Sodom, esteem, wisdom.

014   star, stare, story, straw, steer, store, cedar, cider.

015   stale, stall, steal, stool, hostile, saddle, stole.

016   stage, stash, Swedish, stitch, station, hostage.

017   stake, steak, stick, stock, siding, stuck, setting.

018   staff, stuff, stave, stiff, stove, set-off.

019   stab, steep, step, stoop, stub, stop.

020   sense, since, snows, science, census, essence, swans.

021   sand, sound, synod, cent, snout, Sunday.

022   assinine, sea onion.

023   cinema, cinnamon.

024   snare, snore, signer, sneer, snarl, scenery.

025   snail, senile, sunlight.

026   snatch, singe cinch, sensual, snowshoe.

027   snack, snag, snake, zinc, sneak, snug, sank.

028   sniff, sniffle, snafu, snuff, sinful.

029   snap, snip, snub.

030   seamouse, psalms, seamstress, sums, Samson.

031   housemaid, smote, smite, smith, smut, smooth.

032   summon, Simon, seaman, salmon, cement, seminally.

033   semimonthly.

034   smart, Seymour, smear, simmer, summer.

035   small, smell, smile, Samuel.

036   smash, smashup.

037   smack, smock, sumac, smoke, seeming.

038   semifinal, semifinish.

039   sample, swamp, simple, sympathy.

040   series, sours, Cyrus, sires, source.

041   sort, sardine, sword, assert.

042   siren, surrender, serene, Syrian.

043   serum, sermon, ceremony.

044   swearer, a wise rower.

045   surely, serial, cereal, serialize, sirloin.

046   search, surge, sourish, sergeant, surgeon.

047   circus, circle, swearing, circuit, sarcasm, sorrowing.

048   surf, serve, surface, survive, swerve, survey.

049   syrup, usurp, surprise, surpass.

050   slice, useless, solicit, sluice, zealous.

051   salad, salt, solute, salute, slewed, sled.

052   slain, saloon, saline, slander.

053   slam, slim, slime, slumber, slimy.

054   sailor, salary, seller, celery.

055   slyly, slowly, sea-lily.

056   slash, slouch, sledge, slosh, slush.

057   slack, slang, sleek, swelling, silk, slung.

058   saliva, slave, sleeve, self, sliver.

059   slap, slab, sloppy, slip, sleep.

060   sages, sagas, sieges, suggest.

061   sagittal, sachet, associate, eschewed.

062   session, sessional, suasion, cession.

063   ice jam, sachem.

064   seashore, seizure, sojourn.

065   social, socialite, sagely, seashell.

066   sage judge, sage witch.

067   siege kill, sage call, Sedgwick.

068   house chef, wise chief.

069   sea ship, sage person.

070   sex, six, success, socks, songs, saxophone.

071   squad, scan, soaked, skin, scanty, scoundrel.

072   scan, sicken, skin, scanty, second.

073   scheme, scum, skim.

074   cigar, scar, score, seeker, singer, escort, screw.

075   cycle, icicle, sickle, skull, scale, scalp.

076   Scotch, sickish, sketch, squash.

077 asking, sacking, singing, soaking, squeak, squawk.

078 scoff, skiff, scaffold.

079 scape, scab, scoop, scope, skip, squib, squabble.

080 sieves, sofas, suffice.

081 swift, safety, Soviet, saved, sift, soft.

082 savant, seven, siphon, Savannah, souvenir.

083 Sea foam, sea family.

084 cipher, savor, sever, sphere, suffer, sapphire.

085 civil, Seville, safely, useful, asphalt.

086 savage, sea voyage, sufficient, sawfish.

087 Suffolk, civic, saving.

088 wise fifty, see five.

089 sofa base, safe box.

090 space, spice, spies, spouse, specify, suppose.

091 sipped, spade, speed, spot, spite, spout, spit.

092 Spain, span, spawn, spend, spin, spine, spun, aspen.

093 submit, submarine, submerge.

094 Sabre, zipper, sober, spare, sparrow, spear.

095 spell, spoil, spool, split, spleen, supply.

096 speech, specie, waspish.

097 sipping, sobbing, speak, speck, spike, spoke.

098 soap flake, soup fat, sob freely.

099 wise pope, soap bubble.

1   tea, hut, hood, toe, head, hat, die, doe, eat, hide.

2   Noah, hen, inn, win, knee, awn, wane, wean, wood.

3   may, ham, hem, home, hum, hymn, mow, whim.

4   ray, hare, row, hair, whore, ear, hire, worry, year.

5   law, hole, wheel, awl, eel, halo, heel, hill, lye.

6   jaw, hedge, witch, ash, edge, hush, itch, shy, wash.

7   key, hook, cow, coy, echo, weak, whack, go.

8   fee, hoof, foe, have, fee, huff, wife, wove.

9   bay, hoop, boa, bee, boy, heap, hip, hop, pea, pie.

10   toes, daisy, dice, dose, doze, oats, odds, toys.

11   tot, deed, toad, dad, date, dead, weeded, wooded.

12   tan, den, Dane, ten, dean, down, teen, tin, tune, tiny.

13   tam, dam, dome, dim, dime, team, time, dame, doom.

14   tar, deer, tire, dare, dire, odor, tray, draw, dry.

15   tale, dial, tool, deal, ideal, tell, tile, toil, tall.

16   tissue, dish, ditch, teach, dash, Dutch, touch, douche.

17   tack, duck, dock, dig, dike, take, tag, tuck, took.

18   taffy, dove, thief, thieve, tough, deaf, defy, daffy.

19   tap, dip, tub, dupe, tube, type, deep, top, tip.

20   nose, noose, wines, nice, niece, once, wince, wanes.

21   net, nude, nut, gnat, hunt, hint, node, note, wind.

22   noon, nun, onion, noun, union, nine.

23   name, Nome, enema, numb, enemy, anemia.

24   Nero, winner, Norway, near, owner, narrow, honor.

25   nail, Nile, knell, knoll, null, only, unholy, annul.

26   niche, notch, inch, hinge, wench, haunch.

27   neck, nook, nick, wink, knack, nag, ink.

28   navy, knife, nephew knave, naive, envy, envoy.

29   nap, nip, nape, unbow, unhappy, knob.

30   mass, moose, mess, maze, mouse, amass, amiss.

31   mat, maid, mad, meat, mode, mood, mouth, mud.

32   man, moon, main, mean, men, women, many, money.

33   mamma, mummy, mime, maim, mum.

34   mare, marry, mere, merry, more, moor, mayor, hammer.

35   mail, mule, meal, mellow, mole, mall, Emily, mill.

36   match, mesh, image, much, mush..homage.

37   mike, mug, meek, make, mock, Mecca, Mohawk.

38   muff, movie, move, mafia, miff, mauve.

39   map, mop, hump, hemp, imp, maybe.

40   race, rose, ears, heirs, heroes, oars, rows, rice.

41   rat, rod, read, ride, riot, word, write, red, raid.

42   rain, ruin, horn, rein, run, wren, Reno, renew.

43   ram, room, Rome, rum, worm, rim, harem, arm, army.

44   rear, rower, error, horror, rare, roar, rarer.

45   rail, reel, hurl, oral, rally, roll, royal, rule.

46   rash, roach, Russia, rage, rush, urge, Irish, ridge.

47   rake, rock, rag, arc, ring, rogue, wreck, work.

48   reef, roof, wharf, rave, arrive, rove, rough, arrive.

49   rope, rabbi, harp, ripe, rape, wrap, rub, Arabia.

50   lace, lasso, alias, halos, hills, lease, whales.

51   lot, lid, hold, laid, late, load, welt, wild, healed.

52   lane, lion, alien, Helen, loan, loon, lawn, woolen.

53 lime, lamb, Lima, elm, lime, limb, lame, loom.

54 lair, lure, lawyer, liar, oiler, leer, holler, allure.

55 lily, Lilly, loll, lull, loyal, Lowell.

56 lash, leech, leg, ledge, lodge, latch, Welsh, lush.

57 lake, lock, leak, leg, luck, Luke, lung, log, elk.

58 leaf, loaf, lava, levee, love, wolf, elf, life.

59 lap, lip, leap, lobe, loop, yelp, alibi, elbow.

60 chase, cheese, Jesse, chess, shoes, shows, ashes.

61 chat, sheet, chide, jet, jot, shade, shoot, shout.

62 chain, shin, shine, June, Jane, China, join, ocean.

63 chime, jam, sham, Jim, shame, chum, gem.

64 chair, shore, cheer, jar, jury, shower, usher.

65 Chile, shell, jail, jewel, shallow, shoal, July.

66 judge, choo-choo, Jewish, Joshua.

67 check, chick, Jack, chuck, choke, chalk, joke.

68 chef, chief, chafe, shave, sheaf, shove, achieve.

69 chip, chop, cheap, shape, sheep, ship, shabby.

70 case, kiss, cows, gas, gauze, gaze, guess, chaos.

71 cat, cot, code, gait, goat, gout, guide, kite, Kate.

72 cane, cone, coon, keen, canoe, gun, wagon, agony.

73 cam, comb, come, comma, game, gum, calm, cameo.

74 car, crow, core, crew, cure, gray, grow, cry.

75 coal, coil, cool, gull, keel, kill, clay, gale.

76 cash, couch, catch, gash, gauge, gush, anguish.

77 cake, Coke, cook, king, cocoa, kick, keg.

78 cuff, calf, cave, coffee, cough, cove, cafe.

79 cap, cape, cob, coop, cub, cup, cab, cope, copy.

80 face, fuse, foes, fees, vase, vice, wives, office.

81 fat, foot, fed, feed, feet, vote, evade, fade.

82 fan, phone, fawn, fin, fun, oven, van, vane, Vienna.

83 fame, foam, fume, foamy.

84 fare, fur, fear, fire, four, free, fury, fairy.

85 fall, file, feel, follow, foul, fuel, full, oval.

86 fish, fudge, fetch, vouch, voyage, effigy.

87 fig, fog, fuck, fake, fang, vague, fag, havoc.

88 fife, five, fief.

89 fob, Fab, fib, fop, half-pay.

90 base, pass, bass, bays, boss, boys, hopes, pace.

91 bat, pot, Betty, bed, deed, bite, boat, butt.

92 bean, pan, bin, bone, pen, piano, pony, pun.

93 beam, palm, bomb, boom, opium, poem, puma.

94 bar, pear, Peru, beer, bare, bear, bray, buyer.

95 ball, pail, below, bill, boil, bowl, bell, pill.

96 badge, peach, batch, beach, poach, push, patch.

97 back, peg, bake, beg, pick, pig, poke, book.

98 beef, puff, pave, buff, behave, above, bevy.

99 baby, Pope, pipe, poppy, puppy, papa, peep, pup.

100 thesis, disease, decease, diocese, doses, disuse.

101 Tuesday, attest, deceit, dust, educed, taste, test.

102 design, disown, dozen, descend, dishonor, disinfect.

103 dismay, dismal, dismember, dismiss, dismount.

104 desire, dozer, teaser, desert, deserve, desire.

105 dazzle, docile, tassel, thistle, docile, dislike.

106 decision, discharge, wood sage, wood ash.

107 disk, desk, dusk, tusk, disclose, discolor.

108 adhesive, deceive, disavow, decipher, disfigure.

109 disobey, despair, despite, disciple, disperse.

110 Titus, dates, deeds, dots, duties, tattoos, detest.

111 dated, edited, tattooed, dotted, deadwood.

112 Dayton, detain, tighten, deaden, detonate.

113 diadem, tedium, datum, daytime.

114 Tudor, daughter, editor, theater, tighter, tutor.

115 deadly, detail, tidal, title, total, thoughtless.

116 detach, dotage, deathwatch.

117 dedicate, deduct, detect, detective, idiotic.

118 dutiful, dative, duty-free, a dead fox.

119 tidbit, toothbrush, deathbed, toothpick, tadpole.

120 dance, dense, dunce, tense, twins, tennis, Athens.

121 dint, donned, attend, tanned, tuned, tent, dentist.

122 tenant, Athenian, denounce, two nuns.

123 tenement, autonomy, denominate, dynamo, dynamite.

124 dinner, tanner, tuner, thinner, tinnier, donor, tenor.

125 denial, Daniel, thinly, tunnel, downhill.

126 tinge, tonnage, twinge, Danish, donation, tension.

127 dank, think, tunic, tank, donkey, tonic, dining.

128 tinfoil, tenfold, downfall.

129 Danube, downpour, twin boys.

130 Adams, Thomas, atoms, dames, dimes, teams, thumbs.

131 timid, tomato, tumid, thumbed, admit, deemed.

132 demon, domain, domino, diamond, demand, diminish.

133 damn mad, dumb man.

134 admire, demur, tomorrow, tumor, timer, admiral.

135 dimly, demolish, tumult, tamely, timely, demolition.

136 damage, admission, two matches.

137 teeming, timing, demagog, tomahawk, dooming.

138 a tame fawn, damn fog.

139 Tampa, damp, dump, thump, temple, dimple, tempt.

140 diaries, doors, drays, trace, trees, truce, waitress.

141 dart, dirt, tardy, third, trade, tirade, trout, trot.

142 thorn, train, turn, throne, Darwin, adorn, drench.

143 trim, dram, drama, term, dream, drum, dress, dresser.

144 dreary, dryer, terror, drawer, adorer, trier.

145 dearly, drawl, drill, trail, thrill, trial, twirl.

146 dredge, outrage, thrash, thresh, thrush, torch, trash.

147 Turkey, dark, drake, drug, track, truck, trick, dragon.

148 derive, drive, drove, dwarf, tariff, trophy, turf.

149 drip, drape, drab, tribe, troop, trap, throb, droop.

150 Dallas, atlas, delays, headless, hatless, tales, tiles.

151 adult, daylight, delight, delude, dolt, tilt, tiled.

152 Italian, outline, headland, idleness, talent.

153 dilemma, Talmud, tall mountain, tile man.

154 dealer, delayer, dollar, dweller, tailor, teller.

155 two Lillys, two lollipops.

156 deluge, etiology, theology, tillage, delusion.

157 dealing, delaying, dialogue, dwelling, idling, outlook.

158 outlive, twelve, deliver, doleful, dolphin, telephone.

159 tulip, deliberate, dilapidate.

160 dashes, dishes, ditches, duchess, digest, adjust.

161 attached, dashed, dished, thatched, white washed.

162 addition, adhesion, adjoin, edition, outshine, tuition.

163 attachment, Dutchman, touch her.

164 adjure, dodger, dowager, teacher, thatcher.

165 touch lip, teachless, dish-lady.

166 adjudge, dishwasher, Dutch jewel.

167 attaching, dashing, dodging, teaching, twitching.

168 disheveled, dash over, two chefs.

169 touchback, touch bottom, dishboy, Dutch boy.

170 attacks, attics, decks, ducks, dogs, twigs, tongs.

171 addict, dogged, decade, docket, ducat, tacked, ticket.

172 deacon, taken, thicken, token, dignity, technical.

173 dogma, document, decompose, decamp.

174 dagger, decayer, decree, digger, tacker, tiger, tucker.

175 dingle, ethical, tackle, thickly, tickle, tingle.

176 dictionary, education, dogshit.

177 tacking, taking, tucking, outgoing, attacking, digging.

178 takeover, dock fuel, duck feed.

179 decapitate, teacup, take-up, deck pilot.

180 advice, advise, deface, device, devious, diffuse.

181 David, defeat, deviate, devoid, devote, tuft, typhoid.

182 deafen, define, divine, advantage, adventure.

183 defame, deaf man, tough mama, white foam.

184 Dover, defray, devour, diver, adversary.

185 Devil, defile, youthful, hateful, deflate.

186 thievish, whitefish, deficiency, deviation, devotion.

187 defying, diving, edifying, defect, advocate, difficult.

188 eighty-five, taffy food, tough voyage.

189 a witty fop, deaf person.

190 debase, depose, tapes, tips, tipsy, tops, tubs, tubes.

191 Tibet, adapt, adept, adopt, debate, depth, deputy.

192 deepen, debenture, deepness, depend, dependency.

193 deep mine, weighty beam, witty poem.

194 dipper, taper, tapir, depart, department, deport.

195 deeply, double, table, diplomacy, dipper, dapper.

196 debauch, adoption, a white patch.

197 dipping, tapping, tipping, tobacco, topic, depict.

198 typify, top view, top-heavy.

199 depopulate, top brass, top billing.

200 ensign, insane, unison, insist, incise, incisor.

201 incite, nest, onset, unseat, unsought, unused.

202 insane, unison, unsound, ensign, innocent, unseen.

203 inseam, noisome, winsome, hansom, insomnia.

204 answer, nicer, censor, encircle, insert, insurgent.

205 unseal, insult, nestle, nicely, noisily, unseal.

206 incision, unsociable, new session, noseshine.

207 inscribe, insect, nosegay, unseeing, insecure.

208 insufficient, unsafe, uncivil, insufferable.

209 inseparable, insipid, inspect, newspaper, newsboy.

210 ants, ends, entice, hounds, knights, nights, windows.

211 noted, knotted, united, untidy, indeed, haunted.

212 Indian, entwine, intend, intense, intent, wanton.

213 anthem, entomb, indemnity, nightmare, nutmeg, ointment.

214 enter, entire, winter, entry, hunter, notary, intern.

215 entail, neatly, needle, nightly, handle, indulge.

216 notation, antechamber, untouched, nightwatch.

217 antique, nutcracker, netting, uniting, ending, index.

218 native, endeavor, indifferent, notify, handful.

219 independence, independent, notable, handbag, inaudible.

220 announce, Nancy, annoyance, nuns, onions, enhance.

221 anoint, ninety, ninth, unhand, unwind, unintended.

222 unknown, no noon, no nonsense.

223 anonymous, inanimate, unanimous, no-name.

224 nunnery, un-nerve, new owner.

225 union hall, onion leaf.

226 uninjured, uninsured, a new notion.

227 unknowing, unenclosed, nonequal, nonactive.

228 a new knife, onion flavor, union fund.

229 knee knob, nonbeliever, nonbreakable, nonobedient.

230 enemies, names, unmask, animosity, nemesis, inmost.

231 animate, enmity, inmate, named, unmighty, nomad.

232 inhuman, nominal, nominate, unmanly, unwomanly.

233 unmaimed, unmemorized, unmemorable, new mummy.

234 unmarried, unmoor, enumerate, innumerable, numerous.

235 animal, enamel, namely, nameless, unmail.

236 animation, unmatched, new machine.

237 unmake, anemic, inimical, unaiming, new-make.

238 nymph, unmoved, new movie.

239 nimble, number, unimpaired, unemployed, unimproved.

240 narrows, honors, nurse, owners, winners, nursery.

241 north, honored, inherit, unroot, unread, inward.

242 nearness, unwarranted, near-winner.

243 unharm, norm, unarmed, normal, enormity, Norma.

244 honorary, narrower, honorer, unrewarded.

245 unruly, unroyal, narrowly, enroll, nearly, unreal.

246 energy, enrage, enrich, nourish, ownership.

247 anarchy, narrowing, narcotic, New York, Noah's Ark.

248 nerve, unroof, nervous, unnerve, unrivaled.

249 unripe, unwrap, unrobe, honorable, nearby, unrepentant.

250 annals, knells, knolls, nails, annuals, unlace.

251 enlighten, inlaid, inlet, unload, annihilate.

252 inland, nylon, new-loan.

253 annulment, unlimited, unlimber.

254 inhaler, kneeler, enlarge, enlargement, unlearn.

255 unloyal, nail-hole, Nile lily.

256 analogy, knowledge, unlatch, ineligible.

257 kneeling, nailing, unlike, unlock, unwilling, unlucky.

258 nullify, unleafed, enliven, unlawful, unloved.

259 nullipara, inhaleable, unlabeled, unlabored.

260 hinges, inches, niches, unjust, injustice, unjoyous.

261 enjoyed, unsheath, unshod, unwashed, unwished.

262 engine, enjoin, nation, notion, unchain, ancient.

263 enjoyment, no shame, a new gem.

264 enjoyer, injure, nature, injury, insure, ensure.

265 angel, initial, unusual.

266 unjudged, no judgment, new choo-choo.

267 enjoying, inject, gnashing, unshackle, notching.

268 unchafe, unshaved, anchovy, unshuffled.

269 unship, enjoyable, hunchback, unshapely.

270 Yankees, nags, necks, uncase, winks, next, encase.

271 enact, knocked, uncut, naked, necktie, inactive.

272 encounter, unkind, nickname, naked, nugget.

273 enigma, income, encamp, incomparable, uncomfortable.

274 Hungary, anchor, encore, incur, knocker, winker.

275 angle, uncle, knuckle, nickel, necklace, neglect.

276 engage, inaction, negation, negotiate.

277 knocking, winking, unyoking, knee-kick.

278 uncover, no cuff, unequivocal.

279 innkeeper, uncouple, incubate, incapable.

280 infuse, invoice, infest, novice, knives, nephews.

281 envied, innovate, invade, invite, unfed, unfit.

282 uneven, infant, infantry, inventor, uneven, infancy.

283 infamy, November, infamous, new fame.

284 infer, enforce, infirm, universe, unfair, unfree.

285 naively, inflame, naval, novel, unveil, anvil, unfold.

286 infusion, invasion, unfashionable, inefficient.

287 invoke, infect, infection, navigate, envying.

288 unfavorable, no favorites.

289 enfeeble, enviable.

290 unobserved, knobs, unbiased, knapsack.

291 inhabit, unbidden, nobody, unbought, unpaid, inept.

292 unbend, knee pain, unbind, unbound, unpin.

293 a new poem, nab opium.

294 neighbor, unbearable, inappreciable, unprepared.

295 enable, nebula, nibble, unbowed, unhappily, noble.

296 inhibition, unabashed, new beach.

297 napping, unpack, unpeg, napkin, unbecoming.

298 unpaved, unbehaved, unbefitting, unhopeful.

299 Nabob, unpopular, unpopularity, new pope.

300 Moses, masses, Mississippi, mazes, misses, mosses.

301 amazed, amused, mist, moist, must, mast, mustache.

302 moisten, mason, Amazon, misinterpret, misunderstand.

303 museum, amazement, amusement, Mesmer, mesmerism.

304 amuser, emissary, miser, misery, misrule, Missouri.

305 missile, mislay, muzzle, mussel, measles, muslin.

306 message, massage, mischief, misjudge, mischievous.

307 amusing, amazing, missing, mosaic, Moscow, music.

308 massive, missive, misfit, misfortune, hemisphere.

309 mishap, misbelief, misprint, disbehavior, homespun.

310 mats, modes, mites, moods, moths, mouths, meadows.

311 method, mouthed, immediate, emitted, mediate.

312 maiden, mutiny, mutton, madness, midnight, mutineer.

313 madam, medium, madman, mathematics, my dam.

314 mature, meteor, matron, mother, amateur, mattress.

315 medal, mettle, middle, motley, medial, model, mutilate.

316 mediation, midshipman, midships, mutation, imitation.

317 emitting, meeting, omitting, medical, mitigate.

318 modify, motive, metaphor, midwife, medieval.

319 mudpie, mouthpiece, mutable.

320 meanness, mince, mines, moons, moans, ominous.

321 amount, immunity, manhood, mend, mind, mint, month.

322 minion, eminence, imminent, ammonia nitrate.

323 minimum, monument, monumental, minimal.

324 minor, manor, manner, Monroe, minority, monarch.

325 manly, manual, menial, womanly, humanely, moonlight.

326 manage, management, womanish, mention, moonshine.

327 monk, monkey, mink, mining, maniac, Munich, monogram.

328 manifold, manufacture, manful, manifest, maneuver.

329 monoplane, monopoly, manipulate, menopause.

330 mummies, mammas, mimes, memos, maims, moms.

331 mammoth, maimed, homemade, Mahomet.

332 momentary, moment, momentous, my man.

333 my mom, mime Mary, maim Max.

334 memoir, memory, mummery, memorable, memorial.

335 mammal, mammalove, my mail.

336 mamma shaves, mummy jelly.

337 maiming, mimic, mimicker, mimicked, mimicry, miming.

338 mummify, my move, maim Fred.

339 mumps, mumble, member, membrane.

340 mercy, morass, morose, Morris, hammers, humorous.

341 marred, mart, merit, mirth, myriad, mortuary, murder.

342 morn, morning, mourn, mournful, Marion, marine.

343 mermaid, Miriam, Mormon, murmur, merriment.

344 mirror, hammerer.

345 immoral, merrily, mural, emerald, merely, immortality.

346 march, marriage, merge, marsh, March, marshal, emerge.

347 mark, murky, mercantile, miracle, market, America.

348 morphine, moreover, marvel, marvelous, more fun.

349 marble, morbid, marbled, moribund.

350 mails, males, mills, malls, aimless, miles, malice.

351 melt, melody, mildew, mild, Hamlet, military, mallet.

352 melon, million, millionaire, millennium, melancholy.

353 mailman, emolument, mule master, millimeter.

354 miller, molar, malaria, ameliorate.

355 molehill, may-lily, molehole, Mulholland (Drive).

356 milch, mileage, militia, mulch, malicious, mulish.

357 hemlock, mauling, milk, milkshake, molecule.

358 mollify, malefactor, my life.

359 malpractice, mulberry, malleable, mailboat.

360 matches, images, majesty, magistrate, majestic.

361 matched, mashed, emaciate, much toil.

362 emotion, machine, mission, omission, imagine.

363 matchmaker, immeshment, imagemaker.

364 imagery, major, majority, measure, mushroom, mature.

365 mutual, matchless, Mitchell, much less.

366 magician, my judge, much joy.

367 magic, mashing, matching, magical, Michigan.

368 matchful, my shaver.

369 home shop, match box, my chop.

370 mugs, Mohawks, hammocks, magazine, mikes, makes.

371 mocked, maggot, mugged.

372 mahogany, Mohegan, magnify, magnet, magnolia, magnate.

373 mugwump, make money, meek man.

374 maker, mocker, mockery, mackerel, meager, macaroon.

375 mingle, meekly, mangle, mogul, Mongol, Mongolia.

376 muggish, make wish, makeshift.

377 making, mocking, mike king, mug keeper.

378 megaphone, megaphonic, mock Fern.

379 magpie, amicable, Maccabee.

380 moves, muffs, movies, emphasis, emphasize.

381 mufti, amphitheater, emphatic.

382 muffin, homophile, homophony.

383 movement, move man, movie-moment, my fame.

384 mover, mayfair.

385 mayfly, muffle, muffler.

386 may-fish, my fudge, miffy shrew.

387 moving, Mafia gun.

388 move off, moviefied, my fife.

389 immovable, movable, amphibian.

390 mobs, impassive, impostor, mopes, mops, maps, impose.

391 empty, amputate, impudent, imbued, impute, embitter.

392 impugn, embank, embankment, impend, impunity.

393 embalm, wampum, mapmaker.

394 ember, embryo, umpire, empire, impair, impure.

395 ample, humble, maple, maypole, employ, mobile.

396 ambush, impish, ambition, impeach.

397 mopping, impact, ambiguity, mobbing, mapping.

398 ambivalent, impoverished, mapfinder, mop floor.

399 imbibe, hunchback, mob boss.

400 horses, recess, roses, hearses, resist, irresistible.

401 arrest, erased, raised, harassed, roast, rusty, rust.

402 reason, raisin, arson, horizon, arsenic, resent.

403 resume, wearisome, heroism, reassemble, horsemanship.

404 racer, riser, razor, eraser, reassert, reservation.

405 resolute, resolution, resolve, herself, ourselves.

406 horseshoe, rose hedge, erase chalk.

407 rescue, rascal, Roscoe, risk, rousing, arousing.

408 receive, receiver, rose vase.

409 recipe, rasp, raspberry, respect, horseback, horsewhip.

410 herds, wards, words, rites, rates, radius, artist.

411 righted, redwood, irradiate, irritate, erudite, rotate.

412 retina, ridden, rotten, warden, written, ordain.

413 redeem, rhythm, redemption, rudiments.

414 rider, rioter, retire, rudder, rotary, writer, artery.

415 retail, riddle, ritual, rudely, rattle, hurdle.

416 radish, reattach, reddish, heritage, retouch, hardship.

417 reading, riding, erratic, writing, rooting, article.

418 ratify, ratification, artful, artificial, hurtful.

419 heartbeat, irritable, irritability, redouble.

420 horns, irons, rinse, ruins, urns, harness, ransack.

421 rind, ruined, yearned, warned, errand, around, random.

422 renown, reunion, renounce, reunification.

423 reanimate, renumerate, ornament, uranium.

424 runner, warner, renewer, ironer, ruiner, ironworks.

425 renewal, horn-owl, ran late.

426 orange, reinsurance, range, wrench, ranger, reenjoy.

427 rank, wrinkle, running, raining, yearning, rink.

428 renovate, reinforce, reinforcer, reinforcements.

429 rainbow, rain bath, run up.

430 armies, arms, rooms, rhymes, armistice.

431 armed, remit, remedy, remote, remotely, hermit.

432 remain, Roman, remind, airman, harmony, remedy.

433 remember, remembrance, armament.

434 armor, rumor, roamer, rhymer, rammer, armory, rumor.

435 warmly, wormhole, armhole, harmless, armlet.

436 rummage, armchair, room chest, armchoke.

437 arming, ramming, remake, roaming, rhyming.

438 ramify, remove, ramification, removal, armful.

439 ramp, rampart, rumble, romp, armpit, ramble.

440 errors, horrors, arrears, rehearse, rehearsal.

441 reared, reward, rewrite, rarity.

442 rareness, rear window.

443 rare meat, roar mightily.

444 roarer, rarer, rewirer, rearward.

445 rarely, rural, rurally.

446 arrearage, rerushed, reregister, a rare show.

447 earing, roaring, rearing, hierarchy, reregulate.

448 rarefy, rare fee, reroof.

449 rarebit, rear butt, rear paw.

450 rails, railways, release, hairless, realize, wireless.

451 royalty, world, relate, herald, Harold, relative.

452 reloan, reline, relent, Ireland, reliance.

453 realm, Harlem, heirloom.

454 roller, ruler, railroad.

455 ruleless, roleless, raw ill will.

456 relish, relishment, religion, relation, relationship.

457 warlike, warlock, relic, yearling, railing, reelect.

458 Ralph, relief, relieve, relevant.

459 reliable, relapse, reliability, harelip.

460 ratios, rejoice, righteous, riches, roaches, register.

461 rushed, urged, wretched, rigid, reached, archduke.

462 oration, region, rejoin, ration, Russian, regent.

463 regiment, rich man, reach many.

464 archer, reassure, urger, rusher, Roger.

465 rashly, richly, Rachel, harshly.

466 rejudge, reach judgment, roach jar.

467 raging, airjacket, rushing, reaching, reject.

468 arch foe, airshaft, rejuvenescence, rich family.

469 warship, airship, worship, archbishop.

470 requisite, wrecks, rogues, recuse, rags, recast, works.

471 racket, regatta, rugged, rocket, wrecked, worked.

472 organ, raccoon, regain, hurricane, reckon, rekindle.

473 requiem, argument, workman, war game, recommend.

474 recur, require, ringer, record, rocker, worker, regret.

475 regal, oracle, recall, reclaim, recline, recoil.

476 irrigation, rakish, roguish, aircushion, erection.

477 raking, ringing, rocking, rigging, recognize.

478 recover, recovery, archives, irrecoverable.

479 rock-a-by, rockbottom, rack boy.

480 revise, refuse, wharves, orifice, harvest, refusal.

481 rivet, raft, refit, roofed, horrified.

482 refine, raven, orphan, ravine, revenue, refinement.

483 refamiliarize, warfame, refumigate, air fume.

484 referee, river, rover, warfare, refer, reference.

485 reveal, revolve, revel, rival, rifle, revolt.

486 ravage, ravish, refuge, refugee.

487 revoke, irrevocable, horrific, Irving, roving, raving.

488 revive, revival, reef fish.

489 refabricate, refabricator, reviewable.

490 rubs, rabies, rubies, ropes, repast, herbs, harps.

491 repeat, repute, ripped, robbed, warped, robed, rabbit.

492 reopen, ribbon, repent, European, robin, rebound.

493 airpump, rope mesh.

494 robber, riper, harper, harbor, wrapper, rubber, report.

495 rabble, warble, rebel, repel, repeal, reply, ripple.

496 rubbish, rupture, rapture, eruption.

497 rebuke, repack, rubbing, Arabic, yearbook, Rebecca.

498 rebuff, rubific, rubify.

499 republic, republish, repopulate, airpipe.

500 leases, losses, lasses, Ulysses.

501 leased, least, luster, list, lost, lucid, lowest.

502 listen, license, liaison, loosen, lesson, lessen.

503 wholesome, lyceum, lose money.

504 lesser, loser, ulcer, lessor, illusory, lizard.

505 lazily, wholesaler, loosely, leasehold, leaseholder.

506 lace shawl, loose shoe.

507 lacing, leasing, losing, Alaska, ill sick.

508 illusive, elusive, lice free.

509 lisp, Lisbon, less pay.

510 lettuce, loads, lights, holidays, lattice, ladies.

511 wielded, lighted, loaded, leaded, eluded, elated.

512 laden, leaden, Latin, lightening, latent.

513 ultimate, ultimatum, allotment, ill-timed.

514 ladder, litter, loiter, elder, holder, lottery.

515 little, ladylike, lightly, ladle, wildlike.

516 oldish, late age, lot hedge.

517 leading, loading, halting, eluding, holding, welding.

518 wildfire, old dove, healthful, lotful.

519 letup, hilltop, laudable, holdback.

520 lions, loons, lens, illness, aliens, lunacy, lance.

521 land, lent, lint, lined, alienate, landing, Holland.

522 linen, well known, lenient.

523 liniment, holy name, ill nomad.

524 lunar, liner, Eleanor.

525 lonely, lineal, linoleum.

526 lynch, lunch, launch, lineage, lounge, alienation.

527 link, lanky, leaning, loaning, lining.

528 loan form, loan fee, lone wife.

529 alienable, loanable, loon pie.

530 lambs, limbs, looms, elms, almost.

531 limed, elmtree, limit, limbed, helmet, limited.

532 layman, alimony, alumni, lemon, ailment, lament.

533 Alma Mater, lime mush, lamb meat.

534 hallmark, holy myrrh, hail Mary.

535 limelight, lime oil, lamely.

536 Limoges, illmatched, lame witch.

537 looming, whelming, lawmaker, lime cake.

538 lymph, lame hoof, ill move.

539 lamp, limp, lump, lumber, limber, lamprey.

540 lawyers, layers, lyres, liars, leers, lures.

541 lard, lured, lurid, alert, Lord, hilarity.

542 learn, learned, learning.

543 alarm, allurement, alarm clock, lure money.

544 allurer, lure her, lower/higher.

545 laurel, lawyerly, lair hole.

546 large, lurch, larger.

547 lyric, lark, luring, alluring, lowering.

548 larva, low reef, ill review.

549 larboard, larrup, allurable.

550 lilies, lawless, ill loser.

551 loyalty, lulled, lily white.

552 Lillian, lowland, Lowell Inn.

553 well illuminated, Wilhelmina, loll home.

554 well learned, oil whaler, low layer.

555 lily lover, ill-will howl, loyal Leah.

556 low ledge, holy eulogy.

557 lilac, lulling, ill luck, lolling, owl look.

558 loyal foe, low life, ill liver.

559 lollipop, lullaby, Lilliputian.

560 lodges, ledges, eulogize, latches, luscious.

561 lashed, lodged, legitimate, legitimize.

562 illusion, legion, elusion, elation, legend.

563 lodgment, Welshman, lash him.

564 lecher, leisure, ledger, Algeria.

565 hellishly, lash well, ledge hole.

566 law judge, yellow choo-choo, holy Joshua.

567 lashing, logic, lodging, alleging.

568 well shaven, willowish ivy.

569 algebra, whale ship, yellow chip.

570 logs, lugs, locks, leeks, legs, licks, lax, legacy.

571 locket, locked, liquid, locate, elect, alligator.

572 liken, lagoon, eloquent, elegant, elegance.

573 welcome, alchemy, locomotive, locomotion.

574 licker, liquor, locker, looker, linger, longer.

575 illegal, legal, local, luckily, willingly, alcohol.

576 luggage, leakage, election, legation, languish.

577 licking, lugging, looking, locking, liking.

578 alcove, liquefy, low cuff.

579 lockup, look up, helicopter, likeable.

580 lives, loaves, leaves, levees, olives, wolves.

581 aloft, elevate, lived, loved, levity, lavatory.

582 eleven, leaven, elephant.

583 life mate, love mother, leaf moth.

584 lover, lever, liver, loafer, Oliver.

585 lovely, level, lively, lifeless, lawful.

586 lavish, wolfish, elevation, lavishly.

587 levying, leaving, living, loving, laughing, lifeguard.

588 leave off, ill fever, all five.

589 lovable, alphabet, alphabetize, low pay, aloof ape.

590 lips, helps, ellipse, elapse, lobbies, lobster.

591 lobed, looped, lopped, lapped, halibut, lipped.

592 Alpine, albino, Albany.

593 Alabama, album, elopement, helpmate.

594 labor, laborer, leper, helper, liberty, lubricate.

595 lapel, libel, liable, healing, liability, allowable.

596 libation, low pitch, lip itch.

597 eloping, lapping, helping, leaping, looping.

598 helpful, leap halfway, wallop foe.

599 leap up, elbow whip.

600 juices, Jesus, cheeses, chases, chooses, choicest.

601 jest, joist, Jesuit, chased, just, justice, chest.

602 Chasten, show scenes, chosen, Jason.

603 chessman, jasmine, huge sum, juicy ham.

604 chaser, chooser, cheese rind, chess rook.

605 chisel, jostle, joyously, choicely.

606 cheese shop, choose show, choice age.

607 chasing, choosing, cheesecake.

608 Joseph, cheese filling, chase foe.

609 chessboard, Jasper, cheeseboard, choose better.

610 shades, sheds, cheats, sheets, shots, shouts.

611 cheated, sheathed, shadowed, agitate, Judith.

612 shodden, chutney, chit number.

613 chateau home, aged meat, shod mule.

614 chowder, shooter, shutter, cheater, ashtray, shudder.

615 agedly, shuttle, chattel, shout liar.

616 chitchat, huge ditch, agitation, judicious.

617 jotting, jetting, shading, shedding, shooting.

618 shutoff, shout foul, shoot far.

619 washtub, aged beer, shutup.

620 oceans, shyness, agency, chains, chance, Chinese.

621 giant, gender, joint, shunned, joined, chained, agent.

622 genuine, Shannon, chain enemy.

623 Chinaman, China mainland, Asian hemp.

624 junior, joiner, January, general, generous, general.

625 channel, genially, genealogy, genial.

626 change, chinchilla, ginger.

627 shank, junk, chink, shining, junction.

628 Geneva, show envy, huge navy.

629 juniper, shown hope, chain whip.

630 gems, chemise, chimes, James, chums.

631 ashamed, shamed, geometry.

632 watchman, showman, hushmoney, chimney, gymnasium.

633 Jemima, huge mummy, show mime.

634 shimmer, chimer, shamrock.

635 shameless, chime loud, sham lease.

636 show match, shy homage, wish much.

637 chiming, Jamaica, sumac, shoemaker.

638 shameful, shamefaced, chime factory.

639 champ, champagne, jump, chump, chamber, champion.

640 chairs, Jersey, jars, juries, shears, shares.

641 jeered, chart, charade, shirt, short, shred.

642 shrine, geranium, shorn, journey, churn, journal.

643 Germany, germ, Jerome, charm, chairman, shrimp.

644 sharer, juror, usurer, shearer, assurer.

645 shrill, Shirley, surely, cheerily, churl, shareholder.

646 church, shrewish, cherish, charge.

647 jerk, shirk, shark, shriek, shrug, charcoal.

648 sheriff, cheerful, shrive, giraffe.

649 chirp, sharp, cherub, sherbert, shrub.

650 jewels, joyless, shells, jealous, chalice, Julius.

651 child, jolt, jilt, Juliet, agility, shield, shelter.

652 Chilean, chilliness, Julian, jail window.

653 shyly mate, shell hammer, shoal minnow.

654 jailer, jewelry, jeweler, jelly role.

655 shallowly, jollily, huge wellhole.

656 jolly witch, geology, shilly-shally.

657 shelling, joshing, Shylock, judging.

658 shelf, shellfish, jellyfish.

659 Julep, shallop, agile ape.

660 judges, joshes, chew cheese.

661 judged, joshed, jiu-jitsu.

662 jejunum, Jewish wine, judge Noah.

663 judgment, judgmental, Asia gem.

664 judger, josher, Cheshire.

665 Jewishly, judge well, Jewish law.

666 judgeship, judge Jim, shy judge.

667 judging, joshing, shushing.

668 Judge Ferdinand, Jewish wife.

669 jujube, shoeshop, watch shop.

670 cheeks, jockeys, jokes, jugs, checks.

671 choked, jacket, shocked, jagged, eject.

672 shaken, chicken, jackknife, gigantic.

673 checkmate, chickmeal, jug mouth, edging mower.

674 joker, geography, shaker, sugar, jogger, choker.

675 jingle, jungle, shackle, shekel, chuckle, jackal.

676 ejection, jockitch, joke show, shake watch.

677 joking, shaking, shocking, checking, Chicago.

678 Chekhov, choke ivy, hitching fee.

679 Jacob, checkbook, chalkboard, hitching bar.

680 chives, chefs, chiefs, sheaves, chafes.

681 shaved, sheaved, shift, shoved, shaft.

682 juvenile, shove knee, achieve win.

683 achievement, shame him, shove him.

684 shaver, achiever, Geoffrey, chauffeur, shofar.

685 shovel, shuffle, chiefly, jovial, wishful.

686 Chevy Chase, chief witch, achieve edge.

687 shaving, achieving, chafing.

688 showoff, shove off, huge fife.

689 shaveable, sheafable, chaffable, Java boa.

690 chips, chops, shops, ships, gypsy, gypsum.

691 Egypt, gibbet, shipped, chapter.

692 Japan, cheapen, jawbone, shabbiness, Japanese.

693 shipmate, shopmanager, shipment, chipmunk.

694 jabber, jobber, cheaper, chaperon, shipyard.

695 chapel, jubilee, shoplifter, shapely, chaplain.

696 sheepish, Egyptian, chip shot.

697 chipping, chopping, shopping, shipping.

698 shipful, shopful, cheap fur.

699 shipboard, shipbuilding, shop-happy.

700 access, kisses, excise, causes, excessive.

701 kissed, guest, ghost, accost, accede, custody.

702 cousin, accent, casino, oxen, cosigner.

703 examine, example, exempt, chasm, egoism.

704 gauzier, exercise, exert, exorbitant, geyser, accuser.

705 castle, exile, exhale, axle, gasoline, gazelle.

706 exchange, exchequer, accusation, oxygen.

707 Cossack, accusing, cask, waxing, gazing, exact.

708 cohesive, gasfitter, gasify.

709 gasp, gossip, accept, explain, explode, gospel.

710 kites, quits, coats, cats, gods, goods, goddess.

711 gated, cadet, goaded, quieted, quitted, acquitted.

712 cotton, kitten, kidney, kidnap, goodness.

713 academy, Gotham, gateman, got money.

714 actor, cater, guitar, gutter, quitter, actress.

715 cattle, catholic, coddle, cuddle, kettle, cutlery.

716 cottage, quotation, godchildren.

717 coating, cutting, getting, Gothic, acting, hectic.

718 active, octavo, Octavos, activity, godfather.

719 goodbye, October, equitable.

720 gains, canes, cancel, canoes, guns, wagons, weakness.

721 candy, coined, kind, ignite, count, account, country.

722 cannon, quinine, canine.

723 ignominy, economy, economics, economical.

724 gunner, wagoner, canary, ignore, coiner, ignorant.

725 canal, acknowledge, kennel, keenly, gainly.

726 coinage, conscious, conscience, quench, conjecture.

727 concrete, conquer, conic, cunning, canning, wakening.

728 convey, conflict, convoy, convert, confuse, connive.

729 ignoble. canopy, cannibal, gunboat.

730 combs, chemistry, commas, games, gums, cameos, chemist.

731 combed, committee, comet, commode, commute, comedy.

732 acumen, commune, augment, command, comment, commend.

733 commemoration, commemorate, calm mood.

734 comrade, comradeship, commerce, camera, commercial.

735 camel, calmly, comely, accumulate, accumulation.

736 commotion, commission, commissioner.

737 comic, gaming, chemical, combing.

738 comfort, comfortable, comforting, camphor.

739 camp, compact, combat, compel, gamble, compress.

740 cries, grass, grease, cars, cruise, Greece, cross.

741 cart, carrot, grade, greedy, accord, cartoon, crude.

742 crown, grain, groan, corny, crane, grant, ground, grin.

743 crime, grim, groom, grime, cream, crimson, criminal.

744 career, courier, grower, carrier, crier.

745 cruel, choral, crawl, coral, growl, quarrel, curl.

746 crush, gorge, crouch, grudge, crash, courage, crawl.

747 crack, creak, croak, creek, cork, cargo, character.

748 crave, grave, grief, carve, grove, gruff, caravan.

749 crop, creep, croup, grab, grape, grip, group, crab.

750 glass, glaze, gloss, gales, gills, class, clause.

751 clad, clawed, clot, cloth, clothe, colt, cleat, cold.

752 clean, clown, glen, colony, glean, clink, gallant.

753 clam, climb, column, glean, glum, gloom, claim.

754 killer, color, clerk, clear, collar, glory, clergy.

755 Galilee, clueless, guileless, glow-light.

756 clutch, college, English, clash, collision, collation.

757 clock, cluck, cling, killing, clung, cloak, clog.

758 clove, glove, cauliflower, gulf, cliff, cleave, clever.

759 globe, caliber, clip, clap, club, collapse, eclipse.

760 cautious, cages, catches, gashes, gages, coaches.

761 caged, couched, gadget, gaged, gashed, cogitate.

762 cushion, equation, auction, caution, action, kitchen.

763 coachman, cashmere, cash money, youngish man.

764 cashier, catcher, actuary, cash rate.

765 casual, actual, cajole, cajolery.

766 cash check, coach chess, gauge wager.

767 gaging, catching, gushing.

768 cageful, coyish wife, catch fire.

769 ketchup, catch up, cashbook.

770 cakes, cooks, kings, kegs, gags, cocks, caucus.

771 cooked, kicked, coquette, cocktail.

772 cocoon, quickened, coconut, cognition, quickness.

773 cucumber, gingham, cook meal.

774 kicker, Quaker, acquire, cookery, gangrene.

775 cackle, kingly, goggle, gaggle, giggle.

776 cocksure, quackish, quake shake.

777 kicking, quaking, cooking, Hong Kong.

778 cockfight, cook fish, gang fought.

779 cockpit, eggcup, aching butt.

780 calves, caves, coves, coveys, cuffs, coughs.

781 gift, quaffed, cavity, coveted, covetous, gifted.

782 coffin, given, covenant.

783 caveman, cover model, coffee mug.

784 giver, quiver, caviar, cavern, cover, govern.

785 gavel, calvary, cavalier, wakeful, equivalent.

786 cove shore, coffee jar, cafe chef.

787 equivocal, giving, quaffing, coughing, caving.

788 coffee flavor, cafe food, cough heavily.

789 givable, quaffable, coffeepot.

790 capes, caps, gaps, cubs, cabs, copies, capsule.

791 cupped, capped, Cupid, capitol, captain, captive.

792 cabin, capon, cabinet, occupant, coupon.

793 equipment, cub mother, Cuba yams.

794 copper, caprice, copier, keeper, capper, cooperate.

795 cable, cobble, goblet, couple, gable, cobbler, couple.

796 cabbage, equipage, capture.

797 cubic, cupping, keeping, equipping, coping, Quebec.

798 cupful, cab fare, equip office.

799 copybook, cobweb, capable, capability.

800 faces, offices, vases, vices, phases.

801 vest, visit, feast, fist, fast, vista, faster.

802 fasten, pheasant, fascinate, vicinity.

803 effacement, vasomotor, vase:mantle, vice mayor.

804 officer, visor, viceroy.

805 fossil, fizzle, facilitate, vassal, vessel, facile.

806 visage, physician, hives itch.

807 physic, effusing, facing, fusing, fiscal, physical.

808 evasive, effusive, phosphor.

809 visible, vesper, feasible, offspring.

810 fits, votes, feats, fats, feuds, fates.

811 faded, evaded, fated, fetid, fitted, voted, wafted.

812 fatten, fatness, fitness, evidence.

813 fathom, footman, fight many.

814 father, feather, aviator, fodder, voter, feeder.

815 futile, vital, fatal, fatality, fiddle, fidelity.

816 fetish, fattish, fiduciary.

817 evading, fighting, voiding, feeding, avoiding.

818 fateful, vaudeville, faithful, affidavit.

819 football, avoidable, footpad.

820 fines, fins, ovens, fancy, veins, vines, fence.

821 vend, finite, feigned, faint, fanned, fond, font.

822 finance, financial, fine wine.

823 phenomenon, venom, fan mail.

824 finer, funeral, vineyard, veneer, venerable.

825 vainly, funnel, vanilla, finely, final, finalize.

826 finish, Venetian, vanish, avenge.

827 evening, phonograph, fawning, vinegar, feigning.

828 fanfare, vain wife, fun fair.

829 feignable, finable, finback.

830 fumes, famous, vamoose.

831 famed, fumed, vomit.

832 famine, feminine, foment, effeminate, vehement.

833 view mummy, few moments, Fay mumbles.

834 femur, femoral, ephemeral.

835 female, family, familiar, familiarity.

836 fumage, famish, fumaceous.

837 fuming, fumigate, foaming, fumigation.

838 fame fades, foam free, fume wafts.

839 vampire, vamp, fumble.

840 farce, freeze, first, phrase, verse, fairs, fears.

841 afraid, effort, fort, forty, freight, fruit, fraud.

842 fern, frown, France, French, friend, furniture, front.

843 farm, firm, frame, fireman, former, formidable, form.

844 furrier, forward, friars, fryer, freer.

845 fairly, forlorn, ferule, freely, frail, frolic.

846 fresh, variation, forge, forage, average, virgin.

847 fork, forget, frigate, freckle, frog, freak.

848 forfeit, fervor, fervent, frivolity.

849 verb, verbal, forebear, forbearance, variable.

850 false, fleas, velocity, fleece, veils, fallacy.

851 flood, felt, field, fluid, fold, valet, flout.

852 felon, flannel, feline, felony, flown, fallen, flinch.

853 film, flame, volume, filming, flimsy, flimsiness.

854 flower, flour, flier, flare, floor, valor, failure.

855 filial, flail, valueless.

856 flesh, flush, flash, evolution, foliage, foolish.

857 flag, flake, afflict, flock, volcano, flog, flung.

858 valve, flavor, vilify, fulfill, evolve, velvet.

859 flap, floppy, flabby, flip, flippant, valuable.

860 vicious, voyages, fishes, vouchsafe, officious.

861 vouched, vitiate, fished, fidgety, fidget, fugitive.

862 fusion, ovation, evasion, effusion, aviation, vision.

863 fishmonger, fetch mine, fishmaid.

864 voucher, voyager, fisher, fishery, future, fissure.

865 vigil, facial, vigilance, official.

866 vitiation, fish jaw, half judge.

867 fishhook, fishing, vouching, fudgecake.

868 fishwife, fishfry, vouch for.

869 vouchable, fetchable, voyage back.

870 fogs, focus, folks, efficacy, fox, affix, figs.

871 vacate, effect, avocado, affect, fact, fagot.

872 afghan, falcon, vacant, vacancy.

873 vacuum, folk humor, fake moan.

874 vagary, vicar, vigor, figure, finger, vigorous.

875 fickle, vocal, faculty, focal, vehicle.

876 faction, fiction, factious, avocation.

877 faking, fogging, evoking, Viking.

878 having fought, vague phrases, waiving foul.

879 vagabond, fake pout, vague promise.

880 fifes, fives, vivacity.

881 fifth, vivid, fifty.

882 Vivien, heavy fine, ivy vine.

883 heavy foam, heavy fog, have fame.

884 fever, favor, favorite.

885 five lives, five lambs, vow foul.

886 vivacious, viva! Chile.

887 heavy fog, fife:chord, half faking.

888 vivify, heavy fife, five flavors.

889 viva! Peru, five pies, fife player.

890 fobs, fops, phobias, fibs.

891 vapid, vapidity, vapidly, vapidness, half paid.

892 Fabian, half open, fib unwisely.

893 heavy beam, few bombs, whiff opium.

894 fabric, fiber, vaporize, vapor, viper, vibrate.

895 feeble, feebly, affable, fable, fabulous.

896 foppish, few pages, view beach, wave badge.

897 fibbing, halfback, wave back, heavy bag.

898 heavy puff, Phoebe fair, phobia fear.

899 half-bob, whiff pipe, view pope.

900 basis, abscess, pauses, pieces, pizzas, possess.

901 past, pest, paste, boast, beast, episode, opposite.

902 poison, bison, basin, peasant, business, absence.

903 bosom, basement, pacemaker.

904 opposer, abuser, appeaser, bazaar, absurd, observe.

905 basil, absolve, baseless, puzzle, absolute, obsolete.

906 passage, besiege, beseech, position, opposition.

907 bask, passing, pausing, bicycle, biscuit.

908 abusive, passive, pacify, Pacific, peaceful.

909 passport, pass by, baseball, peaceable, possible.

910 boots, beads, pouts, piteous, pedestal, pedestrian.

911 potato, potted, patted, pitted, bedded, appetite.

912 bitten, bidden, beaten, botany, button, obtain.

913 bottom, epitome, abdomen, epidemic, peatmoss.

914 better, butter, patter, patron, patent, petroleum.

915 beetle, peddle, petal, puddle, battle, bottle, butler.

916 optician, potash, pottage, petition, bootjack.

917 optic, paddock, poetic, pudding, beating, bathing.

918 beautiful, beautify, epitaph, pitfall.

919 bedbug, habitable, hospitable, abatable.

920 beans, bones, pennies, peonies, ponies, Pawnees.

921 pound, band, bayonet, bend, bounty, paint, pant.

922 opinion, peninsula, banana, benign, pinion, opponent.

923 Panama, benumb, bone marrow.

924 penury, panorama , banner, opener, punier, pioneer.

925 panel, openly, penal, penalty, penholder, penniless.

926 bench, bunch, pinch, paunch, banjo, banish, punch.

927 bank, bankruptcy, panic, pink, punning, bunker.

928 bonfire, painful, benevolent, benevolence, benefit.

929 hobnob, pawnbroker, pineapple.

930 Bahamas, beams, poems, pumice, bombs.

931 behemoth, palm tree, balmy weather.

932 Bohemian, bemoan, abomination, abominable.

933 abbey, mummy, ape mammal, happy memory.

934 bemire, boomerang, be merry.

935 pummel, pommel, beamless, bombless.

936 bombshell, bombshelter, opium jaded.

937 beaming, booming, bombing, palming.

938 pamphlet, bomb foe, opium heaven.

939 bump, pomp, pump, Bombay, Pompey, bamboo.

940 brass, brace, breeze, praise, press, prize, purse.

941 proud, port, pirate, period, beard, bird, brat.

942 burn, brine, born, baron, barn, brain, brawny.

943 brim, broom, prime, primary, primitive, paramount.

944 uproar, briar, brewery, prayer, bearer, barrier.

945 April, pearl, barley, peril, purely, apparel, broil.

946 perch, perish, breech, breach, birch, bridge, barge.

947 broke, brook, brick, break, brake, brig, perk, park.

948 proof, perfect, prove, purify, brave, brief, approve.

949 prop, barb, bribe, probe, propeller, purple, parapet.

950 bellows, blaze, bless, bliss, blues, pills, policy.

951 plate, peeled, palate, bloat, blood, blade, belt, bald.

952 billion, plane, balloon, blink, plain, blown, plan.

953 bloom, plum, plumb, plume, blame, plump, blemish.

954 blur, pallor, peeler, player, pillar, appealer.

955 palely, bluely, pale light, pillowless.

956 Polish, abolish, pledge, pillage, apology, bleach.

957 bulk, bleak, black, obliquely, plug, plaque, plague.

958 bluff, bailiff, beloved, belief, believe, Bolivia.

959 pulp, blab, applepie, bulb, palpitate.

960 bushes, peaches, badges, auspicious.

962 option, passion, pigeon, pageant, passionate, patient.

963 bushman, pajamas, pagemark.

964 butcher, badger, abjure, pitcher, poacher.

965 bushel, bachelor, pugilist.

966 happy judge, page edge, boyish usher.

967 pitching, patching, pushcart, objection, object.

968 bashful, pitchfork, apish face.

969 bishop, push-button, poach boars.

970 box, packs, peaks, pecks, pegs, picks, because, epics.

971 packet, picket, bigot, baked, pagoda, peaked, pocket.

972 bacon, begin, begun, beacon, beginner, beckon.

973 become, becoming, pygmy, pigment, bigamy, becalm.

974 poker, packer, pucker, epicure, baker, bakery, bigger.

975 buckle, bugle, pickle, beguile, peculiar, bungle.

976 bookish, baggage, package, picture.

977 pecking, poking, packing, backing, peacock, backer.

978 bagful, bookfinder, beg food.

979 bugaboo, backbone, bagpipe, pingpong, bookbinder.

980 bevies, obvious, beefsteak, behaves, peeves.

981 paved, behaved, buffet, obviate, obviate,

982 buffoon, bovine, puffiness.

983 pavement, beef meal, puff mightily

984 paver, puffer, beaver, before, behavior, beverage.

985 bevel, befall, hopeful, baffle, befoul.

986 peevish, buy fish, pay voyage.

987 puffing, behaving, buffing, bivouac.

988 boy's fife, buy favor, whip fever.

989 puff ball, pave path, buff boot.

990 papacy, poppies, puppies.

991 puppet, bypath, babyhood, baptism, baptist, baptize.

992 bobbin, baboon, Pepin.

993 pipeman, bowing beam, open palm.

994 pepper, piper, paper, peeper, pauper, peppermint.

995 appeal, bubble, pebble, people, pupil, babble, bible.

996 popish, babyish, peepshow.

997 piping, payback, popgun.

998 pipeful, pipefish, pup fleas.

999 baby powder, Bo-peep, puppy pair.

1000 diseases, dioceses.

APPENDIX F

WORD PICTURES OF

THE NUMERICAL ORDER ALPHABET

Samples of Images Which Can be Used as Word Pictures for Your
Numerical Order Alphabet.

Images 1 - 10

Tea (cup)

Noah

May

4. Ray

5. Law

6. Jaw

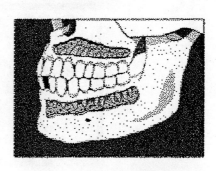

7. Key

8. Fee

Bay

. Toes

Samples of Images Which Can be Used as Word Pictures for Your
Numerical Order Alphabet

Images 11 - 29

11. Tot

12. Tan (shoe polish)

13. Tam

14. Tar

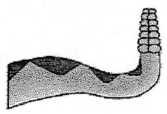

15. Tail

16. Tissue

17. Tack

18. Taffey

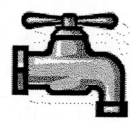

19. Tap

20. Nose

21. Net

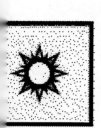

. Noon

NAMETH

23. Name

24. Nero

25. Nail

. Niche

27. Neck

28. Navy

29. Nap

Samples of Images Which Can be Used as Word Pictures for Your Numerical Order Alphabet

Images 30 - 100

30. Mass

31. Mat

32. Man

33. Mama

34. Mare

35. Mail

36. Matches

37. Mic

38. Muff (in)

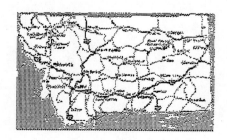

39. Map

40. Race

41. Rat

42. Rain

43. Ram

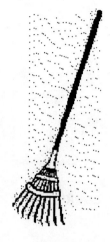

. Rear

45. Rail

46. Rash (medicine)

47. Rake

48. Reef

49. Rope

50. Lace

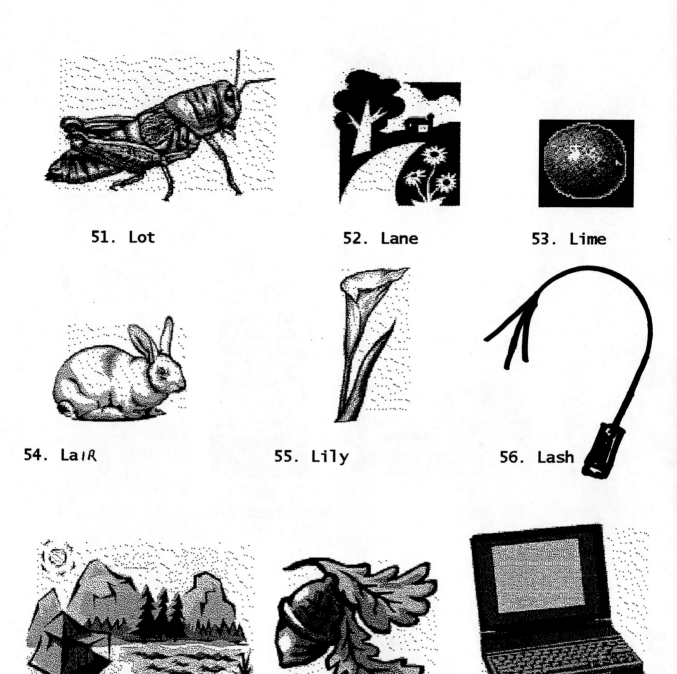

51. Lot

52. Lane

53. Lime

54. La*lR*

55. Lily

56. Lash

57. Lake

58. Leaf

59. Lap (top)

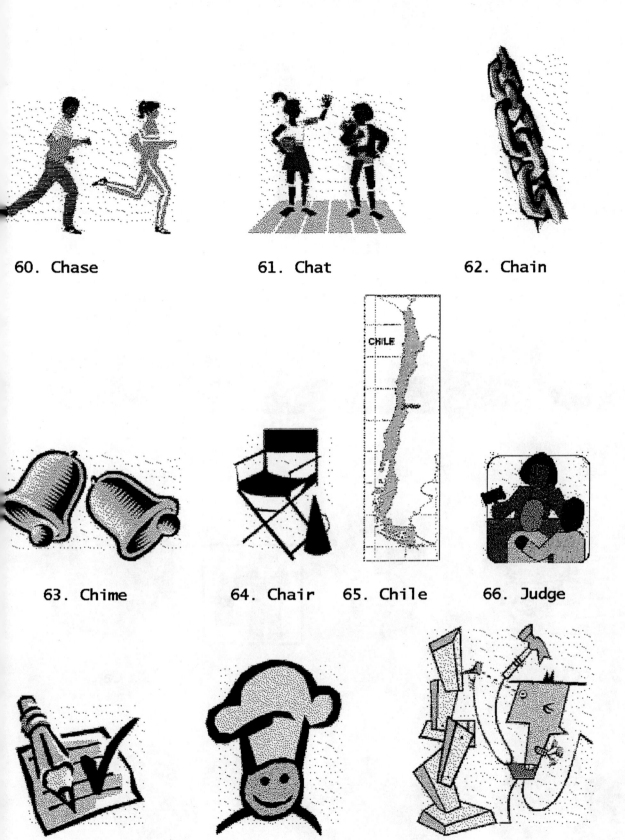

60. Chase

61. Chat

62. Chain

63. Chime

64. Chair

65. Chile

66. Judge

67. Check

68. Chef

69. Chip

70. Case

71. Cat

72. Can

73. Cam

74. Car

75. (made from) Coal

76. Cash

77. Cake

78. Cuff

79. Cap

80. Face

81. Fat

82. Fan

83. Fame

84. Fare

85. Fall

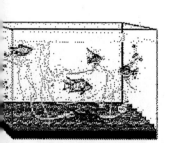

86. Fish

87. Fig?

88. Fife?

89. Fob

90. Base

91. Bat

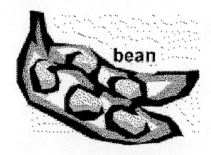

92. Bean

93. Beam

94. Bar

95. Ball

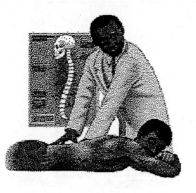

96. Badge

97. Back

98. Beef

99. Baby

100. Thesis

INDEX

Hot flushes and menopause rage,
And memory loss hard to gauge,
I should take it in stride,
And just let it ride,
But it's hell getting old at my age!

Larry Dahl

Wait, There's More!

MiTerre Productions, Inc. offers you a set of four audiocassettes to accompany this book. These self-improvement training products take you step by step as you learn how to improve your memory and to memorize the Numerical Order Alphabet. They are the basis of the seminar/workshops Dr. Amazing presents throughout North America.

Price for each individual volume of the four audiocassettes is $13.98, but you can purchase all four volumes of this training package for only $45.00. Add $5.50 for shipping and handling for a total of $50.50. [California residents add 8.25% sales tax.]

Send your check or money order or your Visa, Master Card or American Express credit card information [with expiration date] to:

MiTerre Productions, Inc.
6221 Wilshire Blvd., Ste 620
Los Angeles, CA 90048

You can also order with credit card via fax at 323-965-0705 or by e-mail at amazingsite@msn.com. If you wish to order by credit card over the Internet, go to www.memorysite.com/books for secured credit card purchasing.

Please be sure to indicate that you are ordering the audiocassette set of LEARN HOW NOT TO FORGET. Include your full name and address for mailing. So that you don't lose your copy, there is no penalty if you tell your friends how to order their own copies.

If you would like to have Dr. Amazing present a memory improvement seminar/workshop for your group or company, check out the seminars website at www.memorysite.com/seminars.

If you would like to have Dr. Amazing present either a memory show or his world renowned hilarious hypnosis show for your group or company, check out his website at www.memorysite.com.

I used to have a photographic memory, but I forgot where I put my film.